FATHER to SON

FATHER to SON

MANLY CONVERSATIONS THAT CAN CHANGE CULTURE

THE STUDY GUIDE

By
Geoffrey Botkin
and Family

The Western Conservatory of the Arts and Sciences
P. O. Box 181
Centerville, TN 37033
www.westernconservatory.org

ISBN 978-1-935877-19-6

Printed in the United States

Table of Contents

HOW TO USE THIS SERIES

This series of conversations comes at the request of many families who asked Geoffrey Botkin how he brought up his five sons. "It took a lot of talking," he recalls, "and that is not easy for a dad and five boys who are quiet and not inclined to be verbal. My sons helped the process a lot when they started asking more questions."

Botkin has discovered that lengthy conversation is integral to the discipling of sons. Sometimes awkward, sometimes lively, sometimes dry, sometimes experimental, and sometimes tentative. The series is an effort to illustrate all these complexities, in a short collection of unrehearsed exchanges between a dad and five sons, all of whom feel a bit uncomfortable about sitting in front of a camera. The viewer must remember that conversations take time. Banter can be quick and colorful, but conversation is rarely economical or colorful. It can appear to be dry and tedious, especially on DVD. But if the viewer will look closely at these long, slow conversations from the point of view of a son, something valuable will emerge.

Even those conversations that appear to be one-sided begin to give the son the assurance that his father cares for him, and the relationship deepens in precisely the ways fathers want their relationships with their sons to deepen. Dads simply need to start talking, and sons need to start listening respectfully and engaging their fathers.

Viewers should note these seven points: Conversations can't be scripted. Conversations take time. Talking is not easy. Long conversations don't sound like the rehearsed and snappy wit of Hollywood writers and actors. Sincere conversation takes discipline. Dads don't have to have perfectly formed ideas and messages for formal conversations. But serious content, even in rambling and spontaneous conversations, can guide sons into a serious relationship with a father that can lead to the kind of spiritual intimacy that builds maturity and character over generations.

Geoffrey Botkin and his sons were willing to record these unguarded conversations in the hope that the exercise can get other men and boys to embark on a similar experience. Serious conversation is never easy. Relationships are never easy. But strong father-son relationships are vital to the survival of the family, the church, and civilization. These relationships begin with the effort and discipline of talking.

VOLUME 1: WORK

LEARNING THE DISCIPLINES OF MANHOOD BY WORKING WITH A FATHER

SECTION ONE: COMMUNICATION

Do we give our sons the kind of instruction that will guide them, preserve them, and give them light for the rest of their lives?

Do we provoke our children to wrath by never giving them the fatherly instruction Scripture commands them to heed?

We fathers need to be walking with our sons day by day. After Moses laid out "the commandments, the statutes, and the judgments, which the LORD your God commanded to teach you," he said:

"And these words, which I command thee this day, shall be in thine heart: And thou shalt **teach them diligently unto thy children**, and **shalt talk of them when thou sittest in thine house**, and when thou **walkest by the way**, and when thou **liest down**, and when thou **risest up**." (Deut. 6:6,7)

This verse is referring to a kind of discipleship that takes place all throughout the day, rather than a few minutes of "quality time" once a week, or even once a day. The biblical model is that we have our sons with us as much as possible, so we can speak into their lives as we live adventures together.

What lifestyle changes will we need to make, to be able to include our sons more in our lives throughout the day?

Psalm 78:2 declares:

> "I will open my mouth in a parable: I will utter dark sayings of old: Which we have heard and known, and **our fathers have told us. We will not hide them from their children**, shewing to **the generation to come** the praises of the LORD, and his strength, and his wonderful works that he hath done."

We must not hide from our children the things the Lord has

done in our lives, the things He has taught us, and the things our own fathers passed down.

We should also encourage our sons to ask:

> "Remember the days of old, consider the years of many generations: **ask thy father, and he will shew thee**; thy elders, and they will tell thee." (Deut. 32:7)

We must teach them to ***value*** everything we tell them.

> "My son, attend to my words; incline thine ear unto my sayings. Let them not depart from thine eyes; keep them in the midst of thine heart. For they are life unto those that find them, and health to all their flesh." (Pro. 4:20-22)

> "My son, keep thy father's commandment, and forsake not the law of thy mother: Bind them continually upon thine heart, and tie them about thy neck. When thou goest, it shall lead thee; when thou sleepest, it shall keep thee; and when thou awakest, it shall talk with thee. For the commandment is a lamp; and the law is light; and reproofs of instruction are the way of life." (Pro. 6:20-23)

How would we train our sons differently, if we considered that we are teaching them to train their sons?

R.C. Sproul, Jr. writes of Psalm 78 ("I will open my mouth in a parable: I will utter dark sayings of old: Which we have heard and known, and our fathers have told us. We will not hide them from their children, shewing to the generation to come the praises of the LORD, and his strength, and his wonderful works that he hath done."):

> "Asaph's message not only passes down from one generation to the next, but is itself the message that must be passed down from one generation to the next. That is, Asaph isn't just telling multigenerational secrets, but the secret itself is, 'Pass it on to the next generation.' This is

> always a critical part of God's covenant. To simply fulfill the immediate demands of the law is never enough. It wasn't enough that Abraham should receive the mark of the covenant. Nor was it sufficient that he should place the mark on Isaac. Rather, Abraham was commanded to teach Isaac to teach his own sons the covenants of God. In simplest form, the covenant God has made with man is simply this: Love, trust, and obey God...and teach your children to do the same. And to take it one step further, we haven't taught our children to do the same unless or until we have taught them to teach their children."
> (R.C. Sproul, Jr. ***When You Rise Up***)

In this endeavor, we should have every faith in success, for Scripture promises that if we "Train up a child in the way he should go ...when he is old, he will not depart from it." (Pro. 22:6)

What if we are not very good communicators? How can we become better?

We should beware of comparing ourselves with men who seem to be better communicators, or seem to "have it all together," if it discourages us from trying to speak to our sons. Moses was rebuked for pleading that he was "slow of speech and of a slow tongue," and "not eloquent" enough to speak forth God's word as commanded (Ex. 4:10). God's response (vv 11,12) was "Who hath made man's mouth? Or who maketh the dumb, or deaf, or the seeing, or the blind? Have not I the LORD? Now therefore go, and I will be with thy mouth, and teach thee what thou shalt say."

We don't have to be perfect communicators before we can do our duty to speak to our sons. All of us will struggle, and all of us must persevere. The effort alone will mean the world to our sons, and the practice will make a world of difference to us.

How do we teach our sons to love Scripture?

The most effective way to teach our sons to love the Bible is to love it ourselves. They need to see their fathers delighting in it, diligently studying it, talking about it, and applying it to their lives consistently. In addition to reading the Bible to ourselves, we need to read it to our families. Leading family worship once a day is not difficult.

What areas of our lives have we not yet conformed to Scripture? In what areas do other things dictate our opinions and decisions?

One of the greatest errors of today's fathers is to fail to apply what they read in Scripture to every area of their lives, and teach their sons to do the same. It has been observed that, two hundred years ago, nearly all men in America, including the unbelievers, were biblically literate and had a Christian worldview; today, even most Christian men suffer from biblical illiteracy and an anti-Christian worldview. This leaves men without a foundation for making righteous decisions, "carried about by every wind of doctrine," and driven by worldiness, fear and pragmatism.

Too often, Christians assume the Bible is silent on the issues that confront them. We know that "All Scripture is given by inspiration of God, and is profitable for doctrine, for reproof, for correction, for instruction in righteousness: That the man of God may be perfect, thoroughly furnished unto all good works." (2 Tim. 3:16,17)

The Bible does speak to all areas of life –child raising, politics, men's and women's roles, education, and the rest – and is our *only* sure guide. We must teach our sons to use it as their "instruction in righteousness," to thoroughly furnish them "unto all good works."

What should we learn from the story of Eli?

The biblical story of Eli has a strong message for the Christian fathers of today. Eli was a religious man who dedicated his life to serving God in the temple, making his family second priority. According to modern thought, God should have been pleased with this. However, because Eli placed his "ministry" above his duty to train his sons in the way they should go (Pro. 22:6) and to restrain them when they consequently did evil (1 Sam. 3:13), God sent upon him a curse "at which both the ears of every one that heareth it shall tingle" (1 Sam. 3:11): "...and there shall not be an old man in thine house for ever... and all the increase of thine house shall die in the flower of their age" (1 Sam. 2:32,33).

Interestingly, even though Eli considered the temple a higher priority than his sons, God accused Eli of "honoring his sons before [Me]," not the other way around.

The grounds on which God was really evaluating Eli was not his temple service, but his family service.

Do we let any things hold priority over our duties to our families?

What are some incisive questions for serious dads?

- Do your sons know what they believe? Do they know the dangers of unbelief?
- Under what circumstances would they die for the faith?
- Do they know courage? To what extent have they been tested?
- Do they know how to confront daily moral tests and triumph?
- Can they defend the faith verbally?
- Can they defend good doctrine verbally?
- Can they articulate a comprehensive statement of faith?
- Do your sons show you proper respect when you lead worship/teaching at home?
- Have you discipled them or neglected them?
- Do you have your sons' hearts?
- Are your wishes and opinions important to them?

- Do your sons want to be with you, or with peers as immature as they?
- Do they receive discipline and instruction with all reverence?
- Do your sons aspire to be godly men or worldly men?
- Do they want to be men of Jerusalem, Athens, or Los Angeles?
- Do your sons have holy affections?
- Do you tolerate insolence or passive rebellion?
- Do your sons have brotherly affection for one another?
- Do they disciple one another constructively or do they act like competitors or enemies?
- Do they fear God in biblical ways?
- How accurately do you represent God to your sons?
- Do your sons delight in your home environment?
- How soon will your family become a Biblical example of a family?
- Do your sons have a vision of patriarchal leadership?
- Do they look forward to being fathers and providers?
- Can you guide and correct them with your eyes?
- Do your children have personal messages they can entrust to others?
- Do they fear God in biblical ways?
- How accurately do you represent God to your sons?
- Will they be ready for marriage and fatherhood at 18? 21? 25? 35?
  Will your sons be trustworthy arrows when you send them forth?
- Can your sons work with you to face any challenge you would put before them?
- How about a family business, with everyone working together?
- Do you know every disciplemaking influence that has alienated your sons from you and your instruction to them?
- Do your sons respect and love the authority and sovereignty of God and his word?
- Can you give your children your blessing knowing they have been trained to be worthy of a blessing?
- Do they see their place in God's providential plan of history?

SECTION TWO: WORK

Why is work so important?

"Therefore, my beloved brethren, be ye steadfast, unmovable, always abounding in the work of the Lord, forasmuch as ye know that your labour is not in vain in the Lord." (1 Cor. 15:58)

The first command God gave to man included the command to work:

"And God blessed them, and God said unto them, Be fruitful, and multiply, and replenish the earth, and subdue it: and have dominion over the fish of the sea, and over the fowl of the air, and over every living thing that moveth upon the earth." (Gen. 1:28)

This is what theologians call the Dominion Mandate: the mandate to subdue and govern the earth as God's representatives on earth. This is the ultimate end toward which we labor. We are reminded throughout Scripture to work diligently, although, as a result of the fall, work was made difficult and painful. The Fourth Commandment includes the command, "Six days shalt thou labor" – many forget that this commandment involves not only rest, but also work. We know that he who does not work shall not eat (2 Thess. 3:10), and a major theme of the Proverbs is exhortation to labor diligently. We must early begin training our sons to work; not only to have the character to be diligent and persevering, but also to see work as a privilege.

Is our own work connected to the biblical purpose of work?

Is work a result of the curse?

As part of being made in God's image, we also have the privilege of working, after His example (Ex. 20:11), and thus there is a holy dignity in labor. Work was not a part of the curse, and the need to work was not a result of sin. R.C.

Sproul, Jr. points out that the responsibility to work "was given in the garden, before the fall. Labor was given as a gift, not a punishment; it must, therefore, be seen as part of the goodness of creation." (R.C. Sproul, Jr., ***Biblical Economics***)

Our sons' sin nature already inclines them to try to get out of work, but the attitude of the day, surrounding our sons on all sides, fuels this aversion to work, and breeds a desire for escape or leisure.

This is in part because, without a biblical purpose for work, man only works out of necessity, to meet his needs. Work becomes a necessary evil. With this attitude, deliverance from work would be seen as a blessing and privilege, and entertainment or idleness would then become a main pursuit in life.

What influences may be teaching your sons that work is undesirable?

The hatred and avoidance of work has always belonged to anti-Christian societies. Of the Greeks and Romans, Rushdoony explains,

> "For them, work belonged to slaves, not free men. In White's summary, 'any free man who dirties his hands with it, even in the most casual way, demeaned himself.' Two friends of Plato who had constructed an apparatus to help solve a geometrical problem were told by that philosopher that they were contaminating thought. According to Plutarch, Archimedes was ashamed of the machinery he had built. Seneca observed that inventions were the works of slaves..." (R.J. Rushdoony, ***Systematic Theology***)

This contempt for labor infected many societies, but young America was built on an entirely different foundation, and owes much of her success to it: the Puritan rediscovery of the nobility of work. Rushdoony writes, "...under the Puritans, labor in one's 'calling' becomes not only the prime moral necessity, but also the chief means of serving and praising God."

The Puritan attitude toward work was still strong in their descendents when Frenchman Alexis De Tocqueville went to America in the 1820's to study and report on the state of this new nation. He was struck by the American attitude toward work, so different from the European disdain toward it: "In the United States professions are more or less laborious, more or less profitable, but they are never either high or low: every honest calling is honorable." The few wealthy American men with no more desire to work would generally go to Europe, "where they find some scattered remains of aristocratic society, among which idleness is still held in honor." (Alexis De Tocqueville, ***Democracy in America***)

Though American men are still known for identifying themselves by their occupations, and not being ashamed of their labor, they are also becoming known for their extravagant pursuit of leisure. Americans are internationally notorious for their insatiable appetite for entertainment, for how much they spend on their "toys," for their expensive vacations, and for listless boredom with the real world around them when the entertainment ceases.

What is the difference between rest and leisure? Should we ever have leisure time?

Our sons should know that there is a place for rest in a life of service, though godly rest differs from today's concept of "leisure."

In ***Systematic Theology***, R.J. Rushdoony writes:

> "The distinction between a Sabbath rest and leisure is a very important one. Leisure is an act of [sinful] autonomy from legal and moral obligations. It is 'time off' from time and history. The world of time is a realm of responsibility,

and leisure activity seeks to escape from obligations. Escapism is thus basic to leisure activity. When men lack a godly calling, leisure has a growing appeal: an opportunity to evade the real world of moral duties, the responsibilities of work, and the realm of accountability. This escapism is stressed heavily by vacation advertising which appeals to the leisure-oriented person. We are told, 'Escape to a tropical paradise,' meaning a humanistic Garden of Eden without work, moral responsibility or law. 'Go now, and pay later,' it is said.

"A Sabbath rest, whether weekly or in the form of a 'vacation,' a poor word and related to 'vacate,' is a cessation of our work in time because of a trust in God and eternity. In such resting, we are confident that the government is not upon our shoulders, but the Lord's (Isa. 9:6), and we can therefore rest because we know our work is governed, guided, and made to prosper in terms of God's providence. There is a triumphant certainty in Paul's words, 'Therefore, my beloved brethren, be ye steadfast, unmovable, always abounding in the work of the Lord, forasmuch as ye know that your labor is not in vain in the Lord' (I Cor. 15:58). Thus to rest in the Lord is not to step or attempt to step outside of time and responsibility but to strengthen our trust that the Lord God makes all things work together for good to them who love Him, to those who are called according to His purpose (Rom. 8:28). Godly rest is an act of ***trust***." (R.J. Rushdoony, Systematic Theology, Vol II

"To rest on the Sabbath day was to remember that man, as a part of God's created order, was totally dependent on the Creator; man's divinely appointed task to have dominion over the created order (Gen 1:26) carried with it also the privilege of sharing in God's rest. The Exodus, too, was a type of creation and thus forms an analogy to the creation account in Genesis." (P.C. Craigie, cited in R.J. Rushdoony's ***Systematic Theology***)

Is boredom in our sons a problem?

On the subject of leisure and escape from work, Rushdoony makes an interesting point especially relevant to young boys:

> "One of the more telling changes in my lifetime is from man's delight in life to boredom. Some years ago, the primary meaning of 'boring' was to drill a hole; to make weary was a minor use and not too common. Today, even children speak of being bored. The world of leisure has created boredom, because it seeks escape from meaning, faith and work.
>
> Not surprisingly, the concept of boredom has revived in civilization as a consequence of the revival of ancient Greek thought. The Greek separation of manual labor from ideas, and of thought from matter, meant that for them creativity was associated with an abstraction from the world. Ivory-tower education is one consequence." (R.J. Rushdoony, ***Systematic Theology***)

What is the difference between boredom, and taking time for quiet reflecting and meditating?

To what extent is boredom a result of an inactive, disengaged mind, lack of interest in the world around us, discontent, and purposelessness, as well as a lack of something to do?

How can we kindle in our sons an interest in real things that will supercede an appetite for leisure and escapism?

Having a desire for accomplishment and a vision for their labor can rescue our sons from aimlessness and boredom. We need to give them a vision for their labor – men should have a purpose to what they do, beyond their needs being met or financial reward. R.J. Rushdoony explains:

> "The goal of work should be godly dominion. Work is not an end in itself, nor is the monetary income it

> produces the goal. The laborer is emphatically worthy of his hire (Luke 10:7; 1 Tim. 5:18); work and pay cannot be separated, but neither can they be equated as though there is nothing more to work than its monetary return. In other words, work is an economic fact, but it must be more than an economic fact. In any society where work is seen simply as an economic necessity and fact, there will be a decline in productivity towards the subsistence level. If men only work to eat (or to play) the meaning and the goal of work soon fades away. As we have seen, work is a moral fact, to be contrasted with theft." (R.J. Rushdoony, ***Systematic Theology***)

When work is not connected to dominion, it becomes a drudgery that can degrade and destroy man:

> "The separation of work from dominion is catastrophic for man and society. It leads to the spiritual sickness of man and to the decline of his culture. It can lead, in some cultures, to the brutalization of man. As man is degraded by his sin and his sinful society into a slave of work whose work is bondage rather than liberation, man responds by aggravating his sin. The response of man to man becomes a form of mutual urges to degrade and defile the other person. ... The exercise of dominion under God is the development of man and the earth by means of work in order to strengthen, prosper, and heighten man's life and service under God. True work and true dominion further life and the potentialities of life. ... The purpose and meaning of dominion is to bring forth the meaning and potentiality, of man, his society, and the earth, and to complete or perfect the God-ordained purposes of creation." (R.J. Rushdoony, ***Revolt Against Maturity***)

How can we always help our sons understand the importance of every task we give them?

Are some kinds of work more spiritual than others?

If labor to subdue the earth under God is a noble duty that He gave to all men, then every means of doing so is equally legitimate, equally noble and equally holy.

> "This then was man's holy calling under God, ***work and knowledge*** toward the purpose of subduing the earth and exercising dominion over it. Thus, ***any vocation*** whereby man extends his dominion under God, to God's purpose, and without abuse of or contempt for the earth God has ordained to be man's domain under Him, is ***a holy calling. The common opinion in every branch of Christendom that a Christian calling means entrance into the ranks of the clergy could not be more wrong. Such an attitude leads to the supplanting of the Kingdom of God by the church, to ecclesiasticism as God's purpose in creation."*** (R.J. Rushdoony, ***Institutes of Biblical Law,*** emphasis added)

This understanding revolutionizes the meaning of vocation. Rushdoony goes on to explain:

> "... a vocation is a ***calling***. The Reformation stressed work under God as a calling or vocation. Since then, however, the meaning of calling or vocation has tended to be restricted. Men think of a ***vocation*** as something professional and a ***calling*** as religious and ecclesiastical. On the other hand, ***work*** has a different kind of origin. It comes from the Anglo-Saxon ***worc,*** and it refers to the exertion of strength to do something. Work is akin to the Greek ***ergon***, work; to ***erdein***, to do, sacrifice; and to ***orgia***, secret rites. As a result, because ***work*** has reference to physical labor, ***work*** has become separated from vocation or calling, a very unbiblical consequence. It must be stressed, therefore, that for us work must be a vocation or calling from God.
>
> "Not only work but life apart from God is meaningless. Work then becomes a question of survival economics,

gaining enough food and shelter to live. For all too many people in history, work has had this connotation. Its goal has been survival, and hence it has had a sad and burdensome aura. Escape from work is then a much desired goal.

"However, in the Bible work is eschatological in meaning. It has a goal, the Kingdom of God. Work can be drudgery, a necessary means of survival, or work can be a means of dominion and subduing the earth (Gen. 1:26-28). ***Work can be a means of maintaining life and no more, or work can be the means of creating the future."*** (R.J. Rushdoony, ***Systematic Theology)***

What kind of tasks and assignments can we give our sons, to let them become part of the dominion-taking mission now?

Should men ever retire from their dominion work? How about taking vacations?

An interesting observation from Rushdoony:

"...while work is not the salvation of man, man ceases to be man if separated from work. Not surprisingly, men usually die within a few years of retirement, at whatever age they retire." (Rushdoony, ***Revolt Against Maturity***)

SECTION THREE: EDUCATION

What is education?

An education can be defined as the training and shaping of the heart, soul, mind, and strength. An education consists not only in the learning of facts and skills, but also in the developing of affections and worldview (our worldview being how we see and judge our culture and the world around us). Anything which affects our worldview and affections – in fact, anything which influences our hearts, souls, minds, or strength – is educational, whether for good or for evil. And this means that all education is inescapably religious.

What is the purpose of education?

In his ***Letters on Practical Subjects to a Daughter***, William B. Sprague summarized it thus:

> "I would have you, then, in the first place, bear in mind that the great object of your education is to enable you to **bring in to exercise the powers which God has given you in such a manner as shall contribute most to His glory.** For all the noble faculties with which you are gifted, you are indebted to the same Being who gave you your existence: on Him also you are dependent for their preservation; and it is a first dictate of reason that they should be employed in His service. ...The object of education then is twofold: **to develop the faculties and to direct them; to bring out the energies of the soul, and to bring them to operate to the glory of the Creator. In other words, it is to render you useful to the extent of your ability."**

What kind of education should our sons have?

According to Rushdoony,

> "It is not enough for boys to be trained to be good; they must also be trained to be able rulers of themselves and of their domain under God." (R.J. Rushdoony, *Systematic Theology*)
>
> "...the purpose of Christian education is not academic: it is religious and practical." Therefore, the kind of education we need to pursue first is the training and shaping that will equip us to do His work comprehensively. (R.J. Rushdoony, ***Philosophy of the Christian Curriculum***)

As we have heard, John Milton declared:

> "I call therefore a complete and generous education that which fits a man to perform justly, skillfully and magnanimously all the offices both private and public, of peace and war."

The kind of education we want to give our sons is not "ivory tower education," removed from the practical duties of a real man's life. They need education to be real men – training that will academically and practically prepare them to disciple other men, to take dominion, to lead their families, to stand in the gates – to be dominion men, family men, church men, statesmen, cultural leaders.

What is the difference between humanist education and Christian education?

Tom Eldredge points out in ***Safely Home***, "The first conflict in recorded history was a battle over education." He explains that Adam and Eve were given a choice between knowing God and walking with Him, gradually discovering more and more of His truth and wisdom; or a shortcut to instant knowledge – to eat the fruit and know everything, good and evil. These two education philosophies – the empty, shallow knowledge centered around man, and the wisdom of God, which comes only through knowing and fearing God – are still at war today. According to Eldredge: "[the Humanist philosophy] emphasizes the autonomous reason of man and his eternal quest for personal philosophy, on the one hand, and social utility as defined by the State, on the other. [The Christian philosophy] emphasizes obedience before God, a key component of which is the development of wisdom and godly relationships."

In ***Foundations of Christian Scholarship***, William Blake writes:

> "Knowledge consists of knowing who God is, who man is, and what the external world is. All learning thus can generally be subsumed under these three categories. The important question is how does man come to know God, the world, and himself? Does one begin with the external world and from there move to God and man? Can priority be ascribed to one avenue of approach over another in this most fundamental educational concern? What entrance does one make into the field of learning? Van Til asserts that God is the completely original and exclusively original personality which serves as the foundation for the meaning of all human predication. Only on this Biblical premise can a pupil know himself or the world he lives in. This is the basic attitude to which teachers must ascribe importance if pupils are to end up knowing anything. Any other approach destroys the Creator-creature distinction which is absolutely fundamental to one's thinking.
>
> "...man must think God's thoughts after Him if he is to know anything. How does one know whether he is thinking God's thoughts? To the extent that God's thoughts are revealed to us in Scripture, to this extent can we think His thoughts after Him.

"Learning and doing are thus intimately linked... Learning is never for learning's sake alone, but at every point it aims to fulfill the divine task given to man. The ivory tower image of university training is thus inconsistent with Christian theism. Academic education and vocational education are not antithetical or even supplementary but necessarily coexist. Learning is never in the abstract, whether it is academic with no task or vocational with no purpose. Learning is doing something in this world – it goes somewhere. Vocation is no less possible without adequate training of the mind, for by development of the intellect man obtains the necessary tool to know God's revealed will and the world he is under command to subdue as God's vicegerent:

"[Quoting Cornelius Van Til] 'The most important aspect of this program is surely that man should ***realize himself as God's vicegerent in history***. Man was created God's vicegerent and he must realize himself God's vicegerent. There is no contradiction between these two statements. Man was created a character and yet had to make himself even more of a character. And so we may say that man was created a king in order that he might become more of a king than he was.'

"Therefore, 'man's project is to build the kingdom of God.' Doing and learning are accordingly inseparable if man is to stand before God as a fully developed human."

How did the educational standards of John Milton's time compare with ours?

John Milton's own education is a lesson in itself – he considered his education still very lacking when he received his MA from Cambridge, and so retired to his father's country homes for six years of intense, self-directed study. He immersed himself in theology, history, politics, philosophy, literature and science – he had already mastered Latin, Greek, Hebrew, French, Spanish and Italian, and went on to learn Old

English and Dutch. His education was highly valued by the leaders and rulers of his time, and he is today considered to be among the most learned of all English poets.

"Seest thou a man diligent in his business? he shall stand before kings; he shall not stand before mean men." (Pro. 22:29)

This was Milton's perspective on how boys should be educated:

> "But here the main skill and groundwork will be, to temper [in] them such lectures and explanations upon every opportunity as may lead and draw them in willing obedience, inflamed with the study of learning, and the admiration of virtue; stirred up with high hopes of living to be brave men, and worthy patriots, dear to God, and famous to all ages. That they may despise and scorn all their childish, and ill-taught qualities, to delight in manly, and exercises for liberty: which he who hath the art, and proper eloquence to catch them with, what with mild and effectual persuasions, and what with the intimation of some fear, if need be, but chiefly by his own example, might in a short space gain them to an incredible diligence and courage: infusing into their young breasts such an ingenuous and noble ardor, as would not fail to make many of them renowned and matchless men."

VOLUME 2: ADVENTURE

LEARNING THE DISCIPLINES OF OBSERVATION AND DISCERNMENT BY HAVING ADVENTURES WITH A FATHER

SEGMENT ONE: ADVENTURE

What part does adventure play in the Christian life?

Life is an adventure. A Christian man should see his life as the mission, the battle and the adventure of taking dominion of the earth (Gen. 1:26, 28) and making disciples of all the nations (Mat. 28:19). We should be able to see even the little things we do, like taking an expedition to the beach, as fitting into the big picture of our overall objective.

One thing we need to do as fathers is help our sons see the things we do together as the adventures they are. This will involve helping our sons interpret the adventures – giving them the foundation to understand what they discover along the way. Whatever they encounter – whether it be sand creatures, evidence of men's mistakes, or pretty girls – they need to be given the foundation to see it through the Lord's eyes.

Think of some examples of common adventures fathers and sons have, and how you can teach your sons to process each adventure.

Trips to the gas station could include instruction on averting our eyes from magazine covers, an afternoon chopping firewood could include lessons about the joy and privilege of dominion labor, and a trip to the woodshed could include a message about God's scourging of those whom He loves, about our need to be turned from our sins, and the path to salvation.

What does it mean for a son to give his father his heart? What would it look like?

Proverbs 23:26 exhorts, "My son, give me thine heart, and let thine eyes observe my ways." The NASB translates it as, "let your eyes *delight* in my ways." God re-emphasizes the importance of this in Malachi 4:6 and Luke 1:17. The turning of the hearts of the fathers to their children and the children to their fathers is a prerequisite for national renewal and blessing, and the failure to do so demands national judgment.

Do your sons understand your ways? Do they know what you believe about all the important issues of life? Make a list of some of the things you need to talk to your sons about this week. What are some changes we need to make in our own lives, to make sure we are setting an honorable and respectable example to our sons? To make sure our ways are worthy of delighting in?

We must be the kinds of fathers whose ways are worthy of being delighted in and emulated. We must train ourselves for the great objectives of Christian manhood, which requires the use of tools instead of toys, and battlegrounds instead of playgrounds. Paul wrote to the church in Corinth, "When I was a child, I spake as a child, I understood as a child, I thought as a child: but when I became a man, I put away childish things." (1 Cor. 13:11) Too many sons reach the age where they need to put away childish things, but then look up at their fathers and see that they have not themselves done that – that they remain perpetual children absorbed in their toys and hobbies.

What snares do fathers need to vigilantly watch out for, that could steal their sons' hearts away? Make a list of outside influences that may need to be checked.

The early teen years are a time when many fathers lose their sons' hearts. Often it becomes apparent that they never fully had their hearts, and when outside influences increased their pull, their hearts were open for the capturing. The most common snares are bad friends (Pro. 13:20, Pro. 14:7, 1 Cor. 15:33), bad media (Psa. 101:3), bad girls (Pro. 6:25,26, Pro. 22:14, Eccl. 7:26) bad activities, etc.)

Why do fathers need to be leaders?

Every father is a leader. Simply by being created as men (1 Tim. 2:13), we have been given the inescapable role of leader, responsible for those under us. This is evidenced in the fact that, though it was Eve who first sinned, "...in Adam all die," – not in Eve (1 Cor. 15:22). Adam was also the one God first confronted after their sin. He was the one held responsible for their fall, because of his original, created role (1 Tim. 2:13) as head, or leader (1 Cor. 11:3). We can lead astray, or shamefully shrink back to let others make our decisions for us, but we are still leading the way by our actions.

What are some ways men are leading badly in their families today?

Examples: Giving over the discipleship of their children to others (Deut. 6:7), yielding to their wives in ungodly ways out of fear (Gen. 16), failing to disciple their wives (Eph. 5:25-27)

What are some ways we can be more proactive in making opportunities with our sons?

Example: Take them along when running errands, exercising, doing odd-jobs; explain things to them during family outings, while watching movies, after hearing a sermon, etc.

What are a father's chief duties to his family?

They can be summed up as **Protection** (Neh. 4:14, Eph. 5:25), **Provision**, (Gen. 3:17, 1 Tim. 5:8), and **Leadership** (1 Cor. 11:3, 1 Tim. 2:11-13).

What are some practical ways we can be preparing even young boys to protect, provide for and lead their future families?

Example: Teaching them to sacrificially look out for their mothers and sisters and anyone who is weaker or in need; teaching them to be diligent and resourceful workers; teaching them to assume responsibility, to be firm-minded and decisive, etc.

Do your sons know why they are being educated? In order to be leaders, our sons will need wide knowledge of many disciplines.

> On the kind of education a man should ensure for his sons, John Milton wrote, "I call a complete and generous education that which fits a man to perform justly, skillfully, and magnanimously all the offices, both private and public, of peace and war."
>
> We should try to impart knowledge of many disciplines to our sons, though it may require a lot of study on our own part. Don't feel like you have to be an expert about something before you can talk to your son about it – it can be instructive to our sons to see us humbly admit our areas of ignorance – but we should at the very least model to them an interest and curiosity in all fields, which will inspire them to study on their own.
>
>> "For the LORD gives wisdom; From His mouth come knowledge and understanding. For wisdom will enter your heart and knowledge will be pleasant to your soul." (Pro. 2:6,10)
>>
>> "I, wisdom, dwell with prudence, and I find knowledge and discretion."
>> (Pro. 8:12)

Think of at least three academic disciplines you'd like to start helping your sons master now.

Do your sons already have academic interests and goals that you can be encouraging them in?

What lessons can we take from the example of Johann Wysse writing *Swiss Family Robinson* for his son?

Two centuries ago German pastor Johann Wysse wrote ***Swiss Family Robinson*** for his 15-year-old son, not only to teach him about nature, exploration, invention, and science, but to inspire him to be a Christian gentleman, to pass his moral tests, and to show him a picture of Christian family culture and dominion-oriented adventure.

What messages are we preparing to pass on to our sons? What kind of a legacy are we preparing for our sons?

SEGMENT TWO: WOMEN

Fathers need to spend a lot of time instructing their sons about girls. A large portion of Proverbs is the voice of a father exhorting his son fervently on the subject of women. This is one of the subjects our sons will likely hear a million mixed messages on by the time they reach their teens – and they need us to teach them to process and judge rightly everything they see and hear.

What are some of the culturally popular views of women that we need to dispel to our sons?

Our sons need to have a biblical view of women. Women are not discardable playthings, women are not lesser beings, women are not essentially evil, women are not imbeciles, and women are not witches.

The Bible tells us that "a virtuous woman is a crown to her husband" (Pro. 12:4), and that her "price is far above rubies" (Pro. 31:10 – wisdom being the only other thing in Scripture which is described thus). Additionally, "whoso findeth a wife findeth a good thing" (Pro. 18:22), and we are told to "rejoice" in our wives (Pro. 5:18). Adam's state without Eve was "not good" (Gen. 2:18) – he was not complete until he had her as the helper in his mission, and the other half of the reflection of God's image and glory. Women are precious fellow creations of God, and men are commanded to "giv[e] honor" unto them, as "heirs together in the grace of life." (1 Pet. 3:7)

How can we teach our sons to show honor to women? Discuss some practical ways they can cultivate and demonstrate respect.

What should we teach our sons about the dangers of women?

We need to recognize that the Bible talks about two kinds of women. In contrast to the virtuous woman, throughout the Bible there are references to the "strange woman" – the woman outside the covenant community, or the heathen woman, sometimes called "foreign women" or "outlandish women." They are women who can, intentionally or not, shipwreck our sons. Scripture speaks seriously of this very real danger.

"And I find more bitter than death the woman, whose heart [is] snares and nets, [and] her hands [as] bands: whoso pleaseth God shall escape from her; but the sinner shall be taken by her." (Eccl. 7:26)

"The mouth of strange women is a deep pit: he that is abhorred of the LORD shall fall therein." (Pro. 22:14)

"For the commandment is a lamp; and the law is light; and reproofs of instruction are the way of life: To keep thee from the evil woman, from the flattery of the tongue of a strange woman. Lust not after her beauty in thine heart; neither let her take thee with her eyelids." (Pro. 6:23-25)

How does Scripture describe the marks of the "strange woman"? How can we train our sons to recognize her?

Examples: flattering speech (Pro. 2:16, 5:3, 6:24, 7:5), ensnaring eyelids (Pro. 6:25), immodest clothing (Pro. 7:10), brazen countenance (Pro. 7:13), loud and rebellious (Pro. 7:11), feet that do not remain at home (Pro. 7:11), etc.

What is the danger of "strange women"? Why does Scripture warn young men away from them so strongly?

What did the arguably most righteous man in the world, the strongest man in the world, and the wisest man in the world have in common? They were all subdued by women. Righteous David became debauched, Sampson was made weak, and Solomon was made foolish, because of weakness for women.

Nehemiah lamented,

"And I contended with them, and cursed them, and smote certain of them, and plucked off their hair, and made them swear by God, saying, Ye shall not give your daughters unto their sons, nor take their daughters unto your sons, or for yourselves. Did not Solomon king of Israel sin by these things? yet among many nations was there no king like him, who was beloved of his God, and God made him king over all Israel: nevertheless even him did outlandish women cause to sin. Shall we then hearken unto you to do all this great evil, to transgress against our God in marrying strange wives?" (Neh. 13:25-17)

Why do women wield so great an influence over men? What weaknesses of ours make us so susceptible to their sometimes-ungodly sway?

What kinds of thoughts should we inspire our sons to think about the young women they see, to put temptation out of their minds?

When Job was pleading his righteousness, he said, "I made a covenant with mine eyes; why then should I think upon a maid?" (Job 31:1 – other translations put it "look with lust at a maid.") Jesus said, "But I say unto you, That whosoever looketh on a woman to lust after her hath committed adultery with her already in his heart." (Mat. 5:28)

We need to teach our sons that there is a way to look at girls which is sinful, and there is a way to look at girls which is commanded – as sisters, with all purity (1 Tim. 5:2).

Our sons need to hear about the right way to look at and think of girls. We shouldn't only teach them what is forbidden, but teach them what kind of thoughts to fill their minds with instead.

How much should we teach our sons about girls and marriage while they're still young?

Scripture gives young men much exhortation on the

importance of choosing a wife carefully. We should start teaching our sons about marriage early, long before girls come onto their radar screen. They need to know about the biblical purpose of marriage, their duties as husbands, and the character of a good wife. Understanding each of these can help keep them undistracted by the wrong kinds of girls and relationships as they get older.

What qualities should we teach our sons to admire in women?

Examples: Submission (Eph. 5:22, Col. 3:18), graciousness (Pro. 11:16), discretion (Pro. 11:22), faith and lack of fear (1 Pet. 3:6), wisdom (Pro. 31:26), a gentle and quiet spirit (1 Pet. 3:4), modesty (1 Tim. 2:9), sobriety (Tit. 2:4), love of home (1 Tim. 5:14, Tit. 2:5), diligence (Pro. 31:13-15), resourcefulness (Pro. 31:16), entrepreneurship (Pro. 31:24), etc.

How do we train our sons to value these qualities in women?

What are some faults we should teach them to look out for?

Examples: Nagging (Pro. 27:15), contentiousness (Pro. 21:9, Pro. 21:19, Pro. 25:24), fear or lack of faith (Gen. 16), silliness (1 Tim. 3:6), gossiping (1 Tim. 5:13), idleness (1 Tim. 5:13), feet that will not stay at home (Pro. 7:11), indiscretion (Pro. 11:22), etc.

A bad wife can drag a man down, and hold him back from going where the Lord wants him to go. What other things keep men from reaching the level they should?

Additional Verses:

Pro 5:3 For the lips of a strange woman drop as an honeycomb, and her mouth is smoother than oil:

Pro 5:4 But her end is bitter as wormwood, sharp as a two-edged sword.

Pro 5:5 Her feet go down to death; her steps take hold on hell.

Col 3:5 Mortify therefore your members which are upon the earth; fornication, uncleanness, inordinate affection, evil concupiscence, and covetousness, which is idolatry:

Pro 6:25 Lust not after her beauty in thine heart; neither let her take thee with her eyelids.

Pro 2:16 To deliver thee from the strange woman, [even] from the stranger [which] flattereth with her words;

Pro 6:24 To keep thee from the evil woman, from the flattery of the tongue of a strange woman.

Pro 6:26 For by means of a whorish woman [a man is brought] to a piece of bread: and the adulteress will hunt for the precious life.

Pro 6:32 [But] whoso committeth adultery with a woman lacketh understanding: he [that] doeth it destroyeth his own soul.

Pro 7:5 That they may keep thee from the strange woman, from the stranger [which] flattereth with her words.

Pro 7:10 And, behold, there met him a woman [with] the attire of an harlot, and subtil of heart.

Pro 9:13 A foolish woman [is] clamorous: [she is] simple, and knoweth nothing.

Pro 11:16 A gracious woman retaineth honour: and strong [men] retain riches.

Pro 11:22 [As] a jewel of gold in a swine's snout, [so is] a fair woman which is without discretion.

Pro 12:4 A virtuous woman [is] a crown to her husband: but she that maketh ashamed [is] as rottenness in his bones.

Pro 14:1 Every wise woman buildeth her house: but the foolish plucketh it down with her hands.

Pro 21:9 [It is] better to dwell in a corner of the housetop, than with a brawling woman in a wide house.

Pro 21:19 [It is] better to dwell in the wilderness, than with a contentious and an angry woman.

Pro 23:27 For a whore [is] a deep ditch; and a strange woman [is] a narrow pit.

Pro 25:24 [It is] better to dwell in the corner of the housetop, than with a brawling woman and in a wide house.

Pro 27:13 Take his garment that is surety for a stranger, and take a pledge of him for a strange woman.

Pro 27:15 A continual dropping in a very rainy day and a contentious woman are alike.

Pro 30:20 Such [is] the way of an adulterous woman; she eateth, and wipeth her mouth, and saith, I have done no wickedness.

Ecc 7:26 And I find more bitter than death the woman, whose heart [is] snares and nets, [and] her hands [as] bands: whoso pleaseth God shall escape from her; but the sinner shall be taken by her.

Pro 22:14 The mouth of strange women [is] a deep pit: he that is abhorred of the LORD shall fall therein.

Pro 23:33 Thine eyes shall behold strange women, and thine heart shall utter perverse things.

Pro 31:3 Give not thy strength unto women, nor thy ways to that which destroyeth kings.

SEGMENT THREE: HISTORY & VISION

We can think of simple activities like building sand castles with our sons as a perfect opportunity to teach them important lessons.

How should we encourage our children to play?

Play is an important part of a child's life. Childhood play is practice for adult life. When children play, they're rehearsing the roles they want to someday fill, and the dreams they want to someday pursue. Play can be very inspirational, and very vision-building, if we instill the right attitudes and ambitions in our sons, and provide them with the right playthings.

What playthings and activities could encourage a godly masculinity in our sons?

Example: to be defenders and protectors of women, to be builders of civilizations, to be creative and resourceful, to enjoy mental and physical exertion, etc.

What kinds of playthings and activities could foster the wrong attitudes in our sons?

Example: to be destructive, to love gratuitous violence, to be consumers, to enjoy mindless entertainment, etc.

What should we think about toy guns? Tinkertoys? X-boxes? GI Joes? Building tree-forts? Playing board games?

One interesting exercise is to show our sons how we can imagine ourselves in historical situations, and then discuss how we would act in the scenario. What would we do if we were 6th century Christians and barbarians were over-running our country? What would we do if we were French Huguenots during the Protestant Reformation? Would we come to the New World? Flee to Geneva? Stay and fight?

Exercises like this give us an opportunity to discuss the ethics of each response, and explain our basis for making decisions. It also gives us a better appreciation of our historical forbears. There are things to learn from every example, both positive and negative.

What positive lessons should we learn from the men of the 6th century? And what warnings can we take from their example?

The main thing we should notice and appreciate about the patriarchs and abbots of the 6th century, and point out to our sons, is that they were men who understood responsibility. They were not only assuming responsibility for their families, but also for their neighbors, and even for the future of their nation in general. This time in history saw cultivation of soil, relationships, discipline, and civility taking place inside these castles.

Leaders are men who take responsibility for others – men who think like shepherds (John 21:15-17). Leaders need to also understand their times, to know what they ought to do (1 Chron. 12:32), to strategize and prioritize wisely. Now is not the time to build castles, and we must not let romanticism carry us away into attractive lifestyles that don't address the needs of this hour.

Who are some good historical role models our sons should know? What are some great examples of Christian heroism they can strive to emulate?

What does it mean to be a prophet, priest and king for your family?

In his sermon "The Great Duty of Family Religion," George Whitefield wrote:

> "And this is apparent, if we consider that every head of a family must look upon himself as obliged to act in three capacities—**as a prophet**, to instruct: **as a priest**, to pray

for and with; **as a king**, to govern, direct, and provide for them. It is indeed true, that the latter of these, their kingly office, is one in which they are not so frequently deficient in, (no in this they are usually too attentive) but as for the former two, their priestly and prophetic office, they often ignore such things. But however indifferent some family leaders may be about it, they may be assured, that God will require of them a proper discharge of these offices. For if, as the apostle argues, "If anyone does not provide for his relatives, and especially for his immediate family, he has denied the faith and is worse than an unbeliever;" to what greater degree of apostasy must he have committed, who has no thought to provide for the spiritual welfare of his family!

"... For if those that only take care of their own souls, can scarcely be saved, what will happen to such monstrous profane and wicked household heads that ignore the spiritual needs of those under their care?" ("The Great Duty of Family Religion," by George Whitefield, 1714-1770)

Have we been providing for our own in all the ways we should be?

What kind of example have we been setting to our sons?

If we could see our sons emulate us exactly with their own future families, would we be pleased with how they governed their homes? Would God be pleased?

Why is it important to teach our sons history? How can an understanding of history help us face the present?

History is one of the most important disciplines we can teach our sons, for in history we see the unfolding of God's plan for mankind. Scripture commands, "For ask now of the days that are past, which were before thee, since the day that God created man upon the earth..." (Deut. 4:32)

As R.J. Rushdoony puts it,

> "History is, like all subjects, a theological study, and in a particularly pertinent fashion. Man lives his life in time and history; to be indifferent to the past and the future is to be ignorant and incompetent in facing the present." (R.J. Rushdoony, ***Systematic Theology***)

He writes,

> "Because the God of Scripture is the Sovereign, the Lord of all creation, history is His creation also. ... According to Acts 15:18, 'Known unto God are all his works from the beginning of the world.' God as Sovereign created all things, their beginning and ending alike, so that history, in all its totality, is the predestined work of the triune God. Past, present, and future are all God's handiwork in their every detail." (R.J. Rushdoony, ***Systematic Theology***)

> "History is the account of man's struggle to play god, and God's providential workings with men as He redeems and redirects them towards the new creation." (R.J. Rushdoony, ***Sovereignty***)

There is no greater or more marvelous adventure than adventuring one's life in service to King Jesus Christ.

What is the great end Christian men should be adventuring towards?

In a parable about His going up to heaven "to receive for himself a kingdom, and to return," Jesus commanded His servants to "Occupy until I come" (Luke 19:13). When he returned, He called them all to account for what they had done in His absence with what He had given them.

> "Then came the first, saying, Lord, thy pound hath gained ten pounds. he said unto him, Well, thou good servant: because thou hast been faithful in a very little, have thou authority over ten cities. the second came, saying, Lord, thy pound hath gained five pounds. he said likewise to him, Be thou also over five cities. And another came, saying, Lord, behold, [here is] thy pound, which I have kept laid up in a napkin: I feared thee, because thou art an austere man: thou takest up that thou layedst not down, and reapest that thou didst not sow. And he saith unto him, Out of thine own mouth will I judge thee, [thou] wicked servant. Thou knewest that I was an austere man, taking up that I laid not down, and reaping that I did not sow: Wherefore then gavest not thou my money into the bank, that at my coming I might have required mine own with usury? And he said unto them that stood by, Take from him the pound, and give [it] to him that hath ten pounds. (Luke 19:16-24)

This was meant as a parable for our instruction, to show us how we are to conduct ourselves in his absence.

What does it mean to occupy until He comes?

Our sons need to understand the objectives they've been given as Christian soldiers. What are our marching orders, and what is the victory we fight for?

"But this man, after he had offered one sacrifice for sins for ever, sat down on the right hand of God; From henceforth expecting till his enemies be made his footstool." (Heb. 10:12,13, see also Psa. 110:1, Luke 20:43, Acts 2:35, Heb. 1:13)

"Then cometh the end, when he shall have delivered up the kingdom to God, even the Father; when he shall have put down all rule and all authority and power. For he must reign, till he hath put all enemies under his feet." (1 Cor. 15:24,25)

From His ascension, to be seated at His Father's right hand, until He returns, His earthly kingdom has been entrusted to us to "occupy until [He] comes," and all His enemies must have been put under His feet and bowed to His authority before He will return.

Before ascending, He left His disciples with these instructions: "All power is given unto me in heaven and in earth. Go ye therefore, and teach all nations, baptizing them in the name of the Father, and of the Son, and of the Holy Ghost: Teaching them to observe all things whatsoever I have commanded you: and, lo, I am with you alway, even unto the end of the world. Amen." (Matt. 28:18b-20)

In His absence, we are to teach His commands to all the nations, spreading His reign and authority to all the corners of the earth, representing His kingly interests as faithful stewards.

This is one of the most important things we need to teach our sons. They must know how to "seek first the kingdom of God" (Matt. 3:36), and to sincerely pray, "Thy Kingdom come. Thy will be done on earth as it is in heaven" (Matt. 6:10). They must learn to see themselves as active agents of His kingdom, reminding the nations of their duty to submit to Him, ready to challenge an entire culture, as the heroes of the Reformation did.

In ***Backward, Christian Soldiers?***, Gary North writes:

> "The Reformation saw the advent of modern printing, and the bulk of that printing was Christian, and by no means limited to gushy devotional tracts. Luther was challenging the whole fabric of Western culture; Calvin was rebuilding his city of Geneva (at the desperate request of the local town leaders); John Knox was winning Scotland to the gospel, using the sword as well as the pen. This literature still survives, even in secular college classrooms; it changed our world. The King James Bible established a standard of excellence in the English language which has never been surpassed. Try to find a modern example of Christian literature that has had this kind of impact!"

What are some practical ways this thinking will affect how we raise our sons?

We live on a battleground, not a playground. What does this mean?

SECTION FOUR: KNIGHTHOOD

How would keeping journals help us?

The purpose of a journal is to record of God's work in our lives. In ***Spiritual Disciplines for the Christian Life***, Donald S. Whitney names some of the merits of journaling as:

- Help in self-understanding and evaluation
- Help in Scriptural meditation
- Help in expressing thoughts and feelings to the Lord
- Help in remembering the Lord's works
- Help in creating and preserving a spiritual heritage
- Help in clarifying and articulating insights and impressions
- Help in monitoring goals and priorities
- Help in maintaining other spiritual disciplines

Edmund S. Morgan makes an interesting historical observation about journaling promoting self-examination:

> "The fact that many Puritans kept diaries of this kind helps to explain their pursuit of social virtue: diaries were the reckoning books in which they checked the assets and liabilities of their souls in faith. When they opened these books, they set down lapses of morality with appropriate expressions of repentance and balanced them against the evidences of faith. Cotton Mather made a point of having at least one good action to set down in his diary on every day of the week." (Edmund S. Morgan, ***The Puritan Family***)

In 1803, Josiah Pratt noted:

> "The practice of keeping a diary would promote vigilance. The lives of many [who do not keep them] are spent at a sort of hazard. They fall into certain religious habits: and are perhaps under no strong temptations. They are regular at church and sacrament, and in their families. They read the Bible and pray daily in secret. But here it

ends. They know little of the progress or decline of the inner man. They are Christians, therefore, of very low attainments. The workings of sin are not noticed, as they should be, and therefore grace is not sought against them: and the genial emotions of grace are not noticed, and therefore not fostered or cultivated. Now, a diary would have a tendency to raise the standard to such persons by exciting vigilance." (Josiah Pratt, ***The Thought of the Evangelical Leaders***)

Is there one best way to journal?

No; every man should determine for himself the most effective way to keep a journal. Some people prefer to keep different journals to record different things.

As part of our journaling, it can be helpful to have a notebook in which we write entries by category. These are the headings the Botkin sons have in their notebooks:

PROMISES AND FAVORITE VERSES
MEMORY VERSES
ANSWERED PRAYER
GOALS FOR MY FAMILY
GOALS FOR MY FUTURE
MEN I'M DISCIPLING
HOW I'M DISCIPLING
MY MESSAGES
FAITH GOALS
INTELLECTUAL GOALS
ACADEMIC GOALS
MY WEAKNESSES; SINS
DISCIPLINE GOALS
FITNESS GOALS
REFORMATION GOALS
MY SPOUSE'S CHARACTER
PRAYERS FOR THE LOST
THEOLOGICAL DISCOVERIES
BOOKS FOR MY LIBRARY

BOOKS I HAVE STUDIED
PRAYERS FOR CHURCH
INTERNATIONAL REFORM
EVALUATIONS AND CRITICISM
MY PROBABLE GIFTS
MUSIC/LITERARY IDEAS
FILM IDEAS
DAD'S MAXIMS

Why must every man have messages?

Every Christian man is called to be an ambassadors and spokesmen for God.

We are commanded to make disciples (Matt. 28:19), to be always ready to give an answer (1 Pet. 3:15), to reprove, rebuke, exhort (2 Tim. 4:2), to proclaim Him (Col. 1:28), and to be heralds of the Gospel (all God's commandments) to our generation.

Every generation is different and faces unique challenges and crises – battle lines change, men forget the law, and new voids and needs arise that must to be addressed. If we are to be effective messengers we will need to have an acute understanding of our times so that we can diagnose the problems, refute the lies, answer the needs, and address the issues.

God has given every Christian man the tools to do this – unique giftings, insights from His Word, wisdom gained from life's lessons, etc. – and we are not to hide what we have under a barrel. We need to be developing messages so that we will have something to say to our crooked and perverse generation.

What are some of our generation's crying needs?

What are some messages that we would really like our generation to hear?

If we could only give one message to this generation, what would it be?

What elements and concepts of knighthood do we need to transmit to our sons?

There is much in the old Christian concept of knighthood that we should rediscover in the training of our sons. The old English word "cnihthad" referred to the transitional period between childhood and manhood. Christians understood that these youths needed to be discipled, and in what ways. The Creator made young men energetic and warlike; therefore this masculine orientation must not be removed by religion, but molded to be constrained by the cause of Christ.

Young men were taught the Biblical morality of life as men, including Biblical aspects of armed defense. These men were expected to be the Lord's officers and ready military leaders in time of crisis. In peacetime they declared war on sin, striving toward holiness in the fear of God. Young knights were not ashamed to be bold about fighting for what was right. The idea of Christian militancy was understood as a necessary biblical virtue. The true youth – the true knight – was a Christian militant.

Disciplined young knights developed militant virtues like prowess, strength, courage, loyalty and perseverance. They also studied the word of God that they might be champions of justice.

This institution of the disciplined warrior gentleman survived for centuries, even after the armoured cavalry became obsolete. One 20th Century historian was searching for a term to describe the great men of modern times and said, "Not all knights were great men, but all great men were knights." (Matthew Bennet, "The Knight Unmasked")

How should we train our sons to be gentlemen?

Confederate General Robert E. Lee wrote:

> "Without a strict observance of the fundamental ***code of honor,*** no man, no matter how 'polished,' can be considered a gentleman. The honor of a gentleman demands the inviolability of his word and the incorruptibility of his principles. He is the descendent of the knight, the crusader, he is the defender of the defenseless and the champion of justice – or he is not a gentleman."

One Robert E. Lee biographer says Lee's own famous greatness of character was part of a family legacy going back to the Norman Invasion of 1066. The Lees were known as brave men for 800 years. That family influence was sustained and improved through the Lee family line all that time. By the 1800s the Lees were established as a family of ***gentlemen***.

Gentlemanly character was the defining ***inheritance*** of the Lee family, and it was valued appropriately and carefully defined as the inheritance was passed to future generations. The Virginia Military Institute's code of conduct drew from the Lee heritage.

Among the other attributes Lee listed, a gentleman…

> "Does not display his wealth, money or possessions;
>
> Does not lose his temper nor exhibit anger, fear, hate, embarrassment, ardor or hilarity in public;
>
> Does not put his manners on and off. He treats people with courtesy, no matter what their social positions may be;

Does not slap strangers on the back nor so much as lay a finger on a lady;

Does not 'lick the boots of those above him' nor 'kick the face of those below him on the social ladder"';

Does not take advantage of another's helplessness or ignorance and assumes that no gentleman will take advantage of him."

Why is the grandest adventure of all being a family man?

The greatest adventure a man can live is to take a wife and together raise many valiant arrows to be fired forward (Psa. 17:4). Families are the building block, the heart, of society. From strong families come strong churches and strong nations. If a man invests in a family biblically, his work will change the face of the world.

Families are also the primary agents of dominion, our true Grand Adventure.

R.C. Sproul Jr., writes:

> "The exercising of dominion over all the created order is the same as making manifest the reign of the kingdom of God over all things. That's what Adam was made for. That's what Eve was made for, to help Adam in this task. And, not surprisingly, that's what the Bride of Christ, the Second Adam, was made to do, to be help to the New Adam as He fulfills His calling.
>
> "What…could be more intimate, more romantic, more dramatic than a shared vision as grand as making visible the invisible reign of Jesus Christ? … It binds us also with our children. While I am raising my children to be soldiers in this great war, I am not raising them so that someday they can be soldiers. Rather, even ***now*** we fight side by side. They do not wait until they are on their own to be about the Lord's business. They are engaged in warfare right now. Every time my children walk together with me

> through the grocery store, every time they remember to say, 'Thank you, ma'am' to the lady behind the counter who gives them a cookie, they are making manifest the reign of Christ. It is not something for later, but something we share in now. Together, as a family, bound together, we pursue the glory of God through making known the glory of His Son." (R.C. Sproul, Jr., ***Bound For Glory***)

If we were exercising dominion in and through our homes, what would our homes look like?

A real Christian home is the incubator of Christendom

The engine for cultural renewal and reformation

The center of dominion and warfare

A powerhouse of discipleship, ministry and evangelism

A refinery of Christian character

A conservatory of the true arts and sciences

A hub for industry and entrepreneurialism

A bastion of Christian culture and godly aesthetics

And a greenhouse for budding Christian leaders.

VOLUME 3: WORSHIP

LEARNING THE DISCIPLINES OF SERVICE IN A COMPROMISED AND RITUALISTIC AGE

SEGMENT ONE: WORSHIP

"The progress and decline of civilization begins and ends with the church and the families which undergird it." Geoffrey Botkin

What questions would you ask your sons to discern their spiritual condition?

Fathers need to check in on how their sons are doing spiritually. What are they learning? What are they struggling with? We should sit down with them often, and ask them questions such as:

What is your biggest concern right now?
What is this doing to you?
What will the future be like if neither of us grow spiritually?
How can Dad help?
What is your responsibility?
What do think the Lord wants the future to look like?
What must we do now, together, to make this happen?

What is the church legacy that our sons have inherited?

What is the church legacy that our sons have inherited? The legacy of the Protestant Reformation included these five "solas," or tenets, the five battle-cries of a great doctrinal cause:

1. Sola Scriptura! Scripture Alone
2. Soli Deo Gloria! For the Glory of God Alone
3. Solo Christo! In Christ Alone
4. Sola Gratia! By Grace Alone
5. Sola Fide! Through Faith Alone

Later, the Puritans desired to carry the effects of the Great Doctrinal Reformation further into the nature and the **life and polity** of the Christian church.

But the grandchildren of the Puritans dropped the ball.

What is the record of ecclesiastical progress and decline in the last half millennium?

16th century: transition from man's doctrine to the doctrines of Grace

17th century: transition from episcopacy to congregationalism among Puritans

18th century: transtition from church/state tyranny/sacerdotalism to personal liberty and healthy family life

19th century: seduction of Christian grandchildren by modern pragmatism and statist neutrality

In the 1820's, Frenchman Alexis De Tocqueville wrote: "The moral meltdown that has overtaken America has been met with a deafening silence from the pulpits of America and the people-pleasing preachers who presume to stand in them. This desolation of decency could not have occurred if the pulpits of this land were once again aflame with righteousness."

20th century: surrender and abandonment of the Kingdom to God's enemies

> "All who are content with a humanistic law system and do not strive to replace it with Biblical law are guilty of idolatry. They have forsaken the covenant of their God, and they are asking us to serve other gods." (R.J. Rushdoony)

Scott Brown points out that the seven "solas" of the modern church represent a worldly regression into compromise:

1. Sola Cultura - let culture define church life
2. Sola Successa - let numerical success legitimize activities
3. Sola Entertaina - let entertainment be the guiding principle
4. Sola Edificia - let the edifice be the center of church life
5. Sola Programma - let programs dominate the people's

time
6. Sola Thralldoma – let the people be enslaved by whatever thrills them
7. Sola Processa – let the church be managed by business philosophies and processes

What is the definition of apostasy?

a·pos·ta·sy

Abandonment of one's religious faith, a political party, one's principles, or a cause. Standing away from. Leaving one's post. Abandoning position.

n : the state of having rejected your religious beliefs or your political party or a cause (often in favor of opposing beliefs or causes) [syn: renunciation, defection] 2: the act of abandoning a party or cause [syn: tergiversation]

How might today's apostasy be described?

False teachers abound, who preach syncretism with an amoral scientific secular state. They also reject the blood-bought doctrines of the reformation in favor of modern superstitions. They tolerate corporate disapproval of families who seek to grow in sanctification. They are reluctant to repent of shallow religiosity and man-centered practices of leadership and growth. Followers of these men and their teachings become idolatrous and unfruitful, continually rejecting the biblical worldview and obscuring the gospel.

If this is the legacy of the 21st century church, how do we as Christian men need to be reforming it?

What record will our sons leave in as the legacy of the 21st century? If we can disciple our sons, it will be the regaining of biblical law and Christian institutions through free homes, free churches, and free nations.

We and our sons are pioneer reformers stepping onto

new ground in a complex century. We are trying to regain surrendered ground so we can take up our positions again.

What does it mean to teach our sons to think like Reformers?

Faithful fathers teach their sons to think like reformers. As Rushdoony points out, "It is not enough for boys to be trained to be good; they must also be trained to be able rulers of themselves and of their domain under God."
(R.J. Rushdoony, *Systematic Theology*)

We should give them a big vision for what this looks like. Even young boys need to know that being rulers of themselves and their domain under God means more than keeping their teeth brushed and their bedrooms clean. The responsibilities we give them as children must point them to their future duty as cultural leaders, with responsibility over a *large* domain.

According to J. Gresham Machen, "The Christian cannot be satisfied so long as any human activity is either opposed to Christianity or out of connection with Christianity. Christianity must pervade not merely all nations but also all of human thought."

As George Grant declares, "Christians have an obligation, a mandate, a commission, a holy responsibility to reclaim the land for Jesus Christ - to have dominion in the civil structures, just as in every other aspect of life and godliness. But it is dominion that we are after. Not just a voice. It is dominion we are after. Not just influence. It is dominion we are after. Not just equal time. It is dominion we are after."

Are our sons at all attracted to the world? Do they wish to be part of it in any way?

If Christians are the leaders in culture, they will not default to the world's ways. They will set the example that the world will follow, as they have done in times past. But if we do not

disciple culture, culture *will* disciple us. There is no middle ground, no zone of neutrality, in this fight.
We cannot let the world disciple our sons. Christian men know that "the friendship of the world is enmity with God... whosoever therefore will be a friend of the world is the enemy of God." (Jas. 4:4) We must teach our sons to "Love not the world, neither the things that are in the world. If any man love the world, the love of the Father is not in him." (1 John 2:15)

If our sons think like Reformers, culture and their peers will hold no sway over them. A Reformer is a shepherd, not a sheep. He is a leader, not a follower. Rather than being attracted to the allure of the world, he will grieve for its sins and set about discipling it. Our sons will have no desire to be part of a world they can see is in desperate need – for their leadership.

While their peers struggle with "fitting in" and "finding their place in the world," our sons will know that their place in the world is this:

To "wrestle not against flesh and blood, but against principalities, against powers, against the rulers of the darkness of this world, against spiritual wickedness in high places." (Eph. 6:12)

"That ye may be blameless and harmless, the sons of God, without rebuke, in the midst of a crooked and perverse nation, among whom ye shine as lights in the world; Holding forth the word of life; that I may rejoice in the day of Christ, that I have not run in vain, neither laboured in vain." (Phl. 2:15,16)

Are our churches defaulting to the cultural norm, or setting the example for the world to follow?

As the nation continues to turn from away God, the church should be at the forefront of the vanguard to combat the turning and lead the nation back to Christ.

Is there something inherently wrong with "contemporary?"

During Benjamin's lifetime, American churches have followed pop trends in church growth and architecture that have conformed church services to popular entertainments of the day, including lights, sounds, and environments that resemble nightclubs or rock concerts.

Are today's plain church buildings, light grids, microphones and electronic music inherently apostate or sinful? No. We cannot call anything sinful which is not identified as sinful in Scripture. It is usually sinful attitudes that create and sustain sinful traditions.

All models and methodologies of ecclesiology must be analyzed carefully according to Scripture. We should not hold to sentimental church traditions simply because they may be familiar, charming, scenic or personally comfortable. A good example is the New England church common in America's godly heritage.

Trends and fads should be examined and made as biblical as possible before they become cultural norms, and carefully analyzed after the fact, as well.

Trying to say one formula for a parish church building is "correct" can be dangerous. Observe the exterior of the perfect, quaint and scenic colonial church, so dear to America's Christian history: Many architectural elements have been embraced as a cultural norm without careful analysis of meaning, function or purpose. The steeple is a sentimental holdover from comfortable cultural landmarks based on the watchtower of the European fortress. The stained glass windows are beautiful holdovers from Roman Catholicism. The Greek façade pays homage to the handsome yet pagan temples of Greece and Rome, right down to the capitals on the columns. The elegance of the permanent structure tended to remove geographic militancy from the local church and focus the community on comfortable allegiance to a local "home church" edifice.

How have both models defaulted to contemporary cultural norms?

The quaint church buildings of the 17th – 19th Century America copied contemporary and popular architecture. Churches were supposed to have a certain "look" which was perpetuated without much departure from tradition.

The present "seeker-entertainment-consumerist-program-driven" model is also perpetuated as a theoretically successful tradition, with little departure from formulas which include worship bands, lightweight sermonettes, and primitive music with simplistic and repetitive words.

How have both models been perpetuated without careful analysis?

Do our sons have a proper understanding of Who God is, and who man is?

What gods do professing Christian men all too often serve? What other gods are we serving?

(Examples: Sports, TV, golf, mammon, cultural relevance, etc.)

Every person is religious. Every man has faith in something, worships something, and bases everything he does on faith in certain beliefs. A man's god can be anything. It can be himself, mammon, government, the passing pleasures of sin… whatever takes the highest place in his life.

Joshua told the Israelites, "And if it seem evil unto you to serve the LORD, **choose you this day whom ye will serve**; whether the gods which your fathers served that [were] on the other side of the flood, or the gods of the Amorites, in whose land ye dwell: **but as for me and my house, we will serve the LORD**." (Jos. 24:15)

The choice before us is not "Should we serve someone?", but "*Whom* shall we serve?" It will either be the One True God, or a rival false god. As Jesus declared, **"**He that is not with me is **against me**; and he that gathereth not with me scattereth abroad." (Mat. 12:30)

There is no neutral zone. There is no theological neutrality. There are no non-partisans in this fight. We must choose this day Whom we will serve.

What is worship? Have we truly been worshiping God in the way that He requires?

Rushdoony explains:"Our Lord identifies worship with obedience to God's every word. The word translated as worship is *proskuneo*, from *pros*, towards, and *kuneo*, to kiss, i.e., to do homage, to submit to, obey, and revere. The meaning of worship is best set forth in Psalm 2:10-12; it means hearing the Son, serving Him, rejoicing in Him, trusting Him, and prostrating ourselves under His authority.

"God requires that all men worship God the Son. Philippians 2:9-11 makes it clear that all men shall bow before Him and acknowledge His authority, either as His people, or as their judge." (R.J. Rushdoony, *Systematic Theology*)

What is the church?

One thing sons should ask about and fathers should explain is the meaning and purpose of the church. What is the church? Rushdoony writes:

"The most common word for the Christian community in the New Testament is *ecclesia*, which can be translated as assembly, congregation, or church. The word comes from *ek*, out of, and *klesia*, a calling. It is a Greek word used in Hellenic politics to describe the coming together of the citizens to discuss the affairs of the city-state, and it is so used in Acts 19:39 by the town clerk

> to describe the Ephesian Assembly. The word thus describes a realm, a state, or a kingdom. The Septuagint uses ecclesia to describe the Israel of God in the Old Testament. The New Testament continues that usage. The church is the assembly or congregation of the called people of God. It is the covenant community of the Messiah." (R.J. Rushdoony, *Systematic Theology*)

Like the family, the church is a training center for Christian warriors.

"And he gave some, apostles; and some, prophets; and some, evangelists; and some, pastors and teachers; For the **perfecting [equipping] of the saints**, for the **work of the ministry**, for the **edifying of the body of Christ**:" (Eph. 4:11,12)

It is vitally important to note that the church is not the Kingdom of God. It is an *agent* of the Kingdom of God, a Kingdom which is as broad as the world. The church is "A local governing body for the multigenerational prosecution of Christ's Kingdom administration," in Bill Einwechter's words, or as he put it more simply, "A regiment in the King's army."

According to Rushdoony, "The *ecclesia* is the *assembly* of those whom Christ governs and who are therefore called to govern the earth under God." (R.J. Rushdoony, *Systematic Theology*)

How should churches train and mobilize "those whom Christ governs and who are therefore called to govern the earth under God"?

(Example: giving all men in the church opportunities to disciple and lead, training up elders inside the church and recognizing them once they are qualified, encouraging the starting of new works, etc.)

Should we train our sons to be clergymen or ministers?

Not professional clergymen, because we need to recover the concept that all believers are priests, and that all men should aspire to shepherd their families and churches. When Geoffrey Botkin speaks of his sons being "ministers," he uses the term in the Biblical sense that all men serve other men as representatives of God, under His authority and in a ministerial capacity, whether they are fathers, church officers, civil magistrates or simply in training these roles.

As disciplemakers, all men serve as ministers, serving God and serving man in Christ's name. Young men need to be doing this conscientiously at very young ages.

SEGMENT TWO: REFORMATION

How do we reform our own churches if there are some weaknesses?

If we are not careful, we will teach our sons to live a dissatisfied, nomadic life in regard to church membership. All men should be respectful observers and wise reformers, being willing to start or support faithful churches in the right places and at the right times.

What characteristics would biblically-ordered churches tend to share? Among other things:

- The faithful preaching of the apostles doctrine
- The right observance of the sacraments
- The faithful practice of church discipline
- A plurality of biblically qualified elders/pastors/overseers/shepherds (not one single ruling pastor)
- The diligent training of men within the church to be family leaders and church officers, emphasizing the development of character qualifications
- The warm inclusion of entire families in corporate worship without dividing or disintegrating families into places or programs of segregation that usurp parental authority or privileges in the teaching of children.

Is it ever acceptable for families to leave churches?

Yes, if those churches and their traditions are destructive of doctrine and families. But reformers can't be disrespectful, destructive revolutionaries.

Christians must not be grumblers and complainers in their churches, nor can they be discontented church-hoppers, who come and go on petty, personal whims.

Any appeal to church leadership to consider any proposed reform or change must be brought with gravity, respect and humility.

Advice to men who must leave questionable churches: If men leave to start more biblically-ordered churches, they must set a good example in leaving: never leave in anger, not in haste, not with slander, never with unresolved problems, but with love and a good testimony to those observing, and as much as possible with the blessing of the leadership.

Further information on church formation can be obtained at The National Center for Family Integrated Churches. http://www.visionforumministries.org/projects/ncfic/

What character should reformers always model to the body of Christ?

"We urge you, brethren, admonish the unruly, encourage the fainthearted, help the weak, be patient with everyone." (1 Thess. 5:14)

"The Lord's bond-servant must not be quarrelsome, but be kind to all, able to teach, patient when wronged, with gentleness correcting those who are in opposition, if perhaps God may grant them repentance leading to the knowledge of the truth, and they may come to their senses and escape from the snare of the devil, having been held captive by him to do his will." (2 Tim. 2:24-26)

Robert Louis Dabney elaborates on the dangers of letting those in opposition go uncorrected:

> "…these misleaders of the people, while you so weakly connive at their indiscretions, may indirectly be preparing the weapon which is to pierce the bosom of fair-haired boy, and summoning the birds of prey, which are to pick out those eyes whose joy is now the light of your happy homes. For your own sakes, for your children's sake, arise, declare that from this day, no money, no vote, no influence of yours shall go to the maintenance of any other counsels than those of moderation, righteousness and manly forbearance."

Are there different kinds of worship? What are they?

As we have seen, corporate worship is only one way men must worship. Scripture shows us four categories of obligatory worship:

1. LORD'S DAY SERVICE (Corporate worship)

"Not forsaking the assembling of ourselves together, as the manner of some is; but exhorting one another: and so much the more, as ye see the day approaching." (Heb. 10:25)

"For where two or three are gathered together in my name, there am I in the midst of them." (Mat. 18:20)

"How is it then, brethren? when ye come together, every one of you hath a psalm, hath a doctrine, hath a tongue, hath a revelation, hath an interpretation. Let all things be done unto edifying." (1 Cor. 14:26)

"Speaking to yourselves in psalms and hymns and spiritual songs, singing and making melody in your heart to the Lord;" (Eph. 5:19)

2. PRIVATE SERVICE (Private obedience and personal sanctification)

"I beseech you therefore, brethren, by the mercies of God, that ye present your bodies a **living sacrifice**, **holy**, acceptable unto God, which is your reasonable service. And be not conformed to this world: but be ye transformed by the renewing of your mind, that ye may prove what is that good, and acceptable, and perfect, will of God." (Rom. 12:1,2)

3. FAMILY SERVICE

"But if any provide not for his own, and specially for those of his own house, he hath denied the faith, and is worse than an infidel." (1 Tim. 5:8)

4. *PRIESTLY SERVICE*

"But ye are a chosen generation, a royal priesthood, an holy nation, a peculiar people; that ye should shew forth the praises of him who hath called you out of darkness into his marvellous light; Which in time past were not a people, but are now the people of God: which had not obtained mercy, but now have obtained mercy." (1 Pet.2: 9,10)

"And hath made us kings and priests unto God and his Father; to him be glory and dominion for ever and ever." Amen. (Rev. 1:6)

One of the great achievements of the reformation was the recovery of the doctrine of "the priesthood of every believer."
Positions of church leadership are open to all men (of qualified character), and even encouraged. "It is a trustworthy statement: if any man aspires to the office of overseer, it is a fine work he desires to do." (1 Tim. 3:1) Rushdoony points out that in the early church,

> "Not only was the physical locale of the church the home, but the qualifications for officers were essentially family virtues, as 1 Timothy 3:1-13 makes clear. The main office, that of *elder*, is the name of the head of a family. Another office, that of *deacon*, is the name for a family servant."
> (R.J. Rushdoony, *Systematic Theology*)

Read the character qualifications for shepherds in I Timothy and Titus 1.

These men are effective disciplemakers in the home and become the rulers in the local churches, which disciple the entire culture every day of the week. Churches can be involved in worshipping and serving constantly in the imparting of a common faith to the population. The church can be teaching businessmen and local magistrates, providing for the deserving poor, caring for widows and orphans, maintaining church courts, training magistrates and future magistrates, and taking over any legitimate duties of health, education and welfare being performed illegitimately by the civil government.

What does *Semper Reformanda* mean? What would it look like in our own lives?

The motto of the Reformers was *Semper Reformanda* – "Always Reforming" in Latin. In one sense, they were referring to their own personal sanctification, to their resolve to be reformed more and more day by day.

"Not as though I had already attained, either were already perfect: but I follow after, if that I may apprehend that for which also I am apprehended of Christ Jesus. Brethren, I count not myself to have apprehended: but [this] one thing [I do], forgetting those things which are behind, and reaching forth unto those things which are before, I press toward the mark for the prize of the high calling of God in Christ Jesus." (Phl. 3:12-14)

> "Therefore leaving the principles of the doctrine of Christ, let us go on unto perfection; not laying again the foundation of repentance from dead works, and of faith toward God, Of the doctrine of baptisms, and of laying on of hands, and of resurrection of the dead, and of eternal judgment." (Heb. 6:1,2)

In another sense, the Reformers were speaking of their mission to reform the culture around them, particularly the church. As the Reformation was waning, in the early 1600's, Puritan pastor John Robinson gave this farewell address to the pilgrims bound for Plymouth:

> "I charge you before God and His blessed angels to follow me no farther than I have followed Christ. If God should reveal anything to you by any other instrument of His, be as ready to receive it as you ever were to receive any truth by my ministry; for I am very confident that the Lord hath more truth and light yet to break forth out of His Holy Word. For my part**, I cannot sufficiently bewail the condition of the Reformed churches, who are come to a period in religion, and will go no**

> **farther than the instruments of their reformation. The Lutherans cannot be drawn to go any farther than what Luther saw, and the Calvinists, you see, stick fast where they were left by that great man of God, who yet saw not all things.**
>
> **This is a misery much to be lamented; for though they were burning and shining lights in their time, yet they penetrated not into the whole counsel of God,** but were they now living, would be as willing to embrace further light as that which they first received."

The Reformation stalled before it finished the work it set out to do. Today we need men who will pick up where the Reformers left off, and give the church and the world a greater and more complete Reformation.

What are some practices of the modern church that must be reformed?

(Example: a bureaucratic clergy class, edifice-based ritual, family fragmentation, etc.)

What is the criteria of a church's success, if not numbers?

What is the sacred-secular distinction? Is it a biblical idea?

The Roman Catholic Church thrived on the idea of the **clergy-laity distinction**: a division between the professional clergy class, and the class of common laymen. This idea is connected to the concept of the **secular-sacred distinction**: that "church" work is sacred, and other work is not.

In this system, Gary North writes, "…priests serve as the unquestioned 'specialists in religion,' while laymen, including elders, serve as the 'secular' hewers of wood and drawers of water. The laymen are specialists in the things of 'the world,' while their priests take care of the spiritual realm. We call this outlook 'sacerdotalism.' (Gary North, *Backward, Christian Soldiers?*)

Sacerdotalism ignores the fact that "The earth is the LORD'S, and the fulness thereof; the world, and they that dwell therein." (Psa. 24:1, Psa. 89:11, 1 Cor. 10:26) As Abraham Kuyper puts it, "In the total expanse of human life there is not a single square inch of which the Christ, who alone is sovereign, does not declare, 'That is mine!'"

If there is no secular-sacred distinction, does this mean that every field of labor is a place for Kingdom work? That Christians are required to take dominion of them all?

Because every area of life and labor belongs to Him, all should be governed in His name and according to His principles. So, to exercise dominion in *any* sphere in His name is holy work – and it is commanded work.

Rushdoony says, "No more than the Romans could lock up Jesus Christ inside a sealed tomb can the churchmen of our day confine Him to the church. If they continue to try to lock Him into the church, He will shatter the church as He did the tomb, and leave it empty as He emerges to rule the world, for He 'is the blessed and only Potentate, the King of kings, and Lord of lords' (1 Tim. 6:15)." (R.J. Rushdoony, *Sovereignty*)

Historian John Chalfont described the sacerdotalism of modern evangelicalism this way:

> "The Abandonment Theology of today's evangelicalism describes a faith which deceptively pawns itself off as Christianity by operating in the name of Christ, but which produces fruits destructive to America's God-given freedoms. It comprises what is left today of the militant, power- filled, full-dimensional Christian faith of America's Founders after decades of erosion, watering down and trivializing of God's action mandates by America's Abandonment Clergy. It is a "feel good"

theology that patronizes Jesus Christ and thereby gains legitimacy, while at the same time produces disobedience to the commands of God and desertion of Christian duty. It is at home in the world and seeks its legitimacy from a rival deity called the state."

SEGMENT THREE: MUSIC

What is wrong with most worship services today?

Many "worship services" have turned into a time to worship the creature rather than the creator. Many churches have become more like circuses, country clubs, entertainment venues, oprylands, coffeehouses, therapy clinics, daycare centers, and/or local chapters of the public school cartel, than churches. It's not just the architecture of the building, it's the architecture of the service. Some of these are replacing the name 'church' with "Worship Center."

How can we teach our sons what emotions are lawful or unlawful? How can we teach them to control their emotions biblically?

In the last century, our culture has become increasingly dedicated to the idea that music or art created in a state of high emotionalism and intellectual emptiness is superior to music or art created through the traditional means of study and hard work. These "artists" glorify the natural impulse over the application of the fully-engaged mind.

Christians, however, should not give pre-eminence to their "spontaneous emotional impulse." For one thing, we have been commanded to "take every thought captive to the obedience of Christ" (2 Cor 10:5). This is a gradual process of continual reformation of every aspect of our lives – progressive sanctification. And if we do not take every thought captive to the obedience of Christ, we can be certain that every thought will be taken captive to the obedience of something else.

Second, man has inherited a sin nature, so the natural state of his thoughts, deeds, actions and emotions are sinful (Jer. 17:9, Psa. 14:1,3, Psa. 53:1, Psa. 53:3, Ecc. 7:20, Rom. 3:12, Rom. 3:23). Man cannot take every thought captive if he is exchanging his (commanded) spirit of constant, self-conscious analysis for a (natural) spirit of uncontrolled indulgence of his natural desires and impulses.

Do we know what kind of music our sons are listening to, and what affect it may be having on them?

Nothing, not even music, is neutral. It either exalts God's order or man's selfish design. Every musical and artistic expression is a form of communication; even the pure, simple sounds produced by an instrument can evoke feelings and ideas and do convey meaning.

While there may be nothing inherently evil in any particular instrument or the sound it makes, sinful or selfish attitudes of the musician or composer can defile the music and its hearers.

The great theologian John Calvin understood that music could communicate strong moral messages and was a powerful disciple-making influence. He wrote,

> "Among all the other things that are proper for the recreation of man and for giving him pleasure, music, if not the first, is among the most important; and we must consider it a gift from God expressly made for that purpose. And for this reason we must be all the more careful not to abuse it, for fear of defiling or contaminating it, converting to our damnation what is intended for our profit and salvation. If even for this reason alone, we might well be moved to restrict the use of music to make it serve only what is respectable and never use it for unbridled dissipations or for emasculating ourselves with immoderate pleasure. Nor should it lead us to lasciviousness or shamelessness.
>
> "...We find from experience that it has an insidious and well-nigh incredible power to move us whither it will. And for this reason we must be all the more diligent to control music in such a way that it will serve us for good and

in no way harm us. This is why the early doctors of the church used to complain that the people of their time were addicted to illicit and shameless songs, which they were right to call a mortal, world-corrupting poison of Satan's." (From Calvin's Preface to the Geneva Psalter of 1543)

What can we and our sons learn from the examples of men like Bach?

Johann Sebastian Bach was born in 1685 into one of the most prestigious and influential family lines in history. For nearly 300 years the Bach family dominated the musical world in Germany to such a degree that according to some scholars, "At times the word Bach became synonymous with musician..." Johann was a visionary father who appreciated his strong heritage and raised his twenty children to continue the musical dynasty. He was also a staunch Lutheran and one of the best examples we have of a man who tirelessly exercised his God given gifts and inheritance to reach new heights of musical excellence and harmonic perfection. In his own words, his efforts were "For the glory of the most high God alone, and for my neighbor to learn from."

According to historian Paul Johnson:

> "Bach was by far the most hardworking of the great musicians, taking huge pains with everything he did.... It is impossible to find, in any of his scores, time-serving repetitions, shortcuts, carelessness, or even the smallest hint of vulgarity...
>
> "[H]is Christianity took the primary form of worshipping God through sound. That sound, whether performed by himself or others, had to be of the highest quality, always and everywhere. Anything less would be an insult to the Deity, or at best, a gross dereliction of duty. Moreover, quality was not enough. Bach was aware of the great originality of his mind both in devising new musical forms and perfecting old ones."
> (Paul Johnson, *The Creators*)

How do God's principles of order apply to other areas of creativity, such as architecture, graphic design, or filmmaking?

Because we were made in the image of God, the Creator, we are also creators. However, we cannot create with complete originality, as God did – creating something *ex nihilo*, out of nothing.

> The thing that hath been, it is that which shall be; and that which is done is that which shall be done: and there is no new thing under the sun. Is there any thing whereof it may be said, See, this is new? It hath been already of old time, which was before us. (Ecc. 1:9-10)

To act on the presumption that we have the ability to create from scratch is to act in rebellion – and to act in vain. Interestingly, many of the artists, musicians and philosophers who claimed the capacity for new and original thought and creation (making something of nothing), ended up exalting the nothing. Avant-garde composer John Cage, pioneer of "chance music" and other forms of non-music, wrote:

"I have nothing to say / and I am saying it /
and that is poetry / as I needed it."

Our mission is to take dominion of what already exists, using the laws and ordinances that God has given us. Like Bach, we must discipline ourselves and strive for excellence as we explore and discover. Like Bach we must always be perfecting, reforming and struggling to reach new heights of accomplishment for the glory of God.

What are some of the biblical principals that can be applied to music?

"Let all things be done decently and in order." (1Cor. 14:40)

"For God is not the author of confusion, but of peace, as in all churches of the saints." (1Cor. 14:33)

"Finally, brethren, whatsoever things are true, whatsoever things are honest, whatsoever things are just, whatsoever things are pure, whatsoever things are lovely, whatsoever things are of good report; if there be any virtue, and if there be any praise, think on these things." (Phl. 4:8)

What are our sons learning from us about their worship and religious duties?

All fathers teach their sons about worship and religious duties. Most sons learn from their fathers that the sum total of their church duty is to sit in a pew each week, put money in the collection plate, pretend to be 'touched' by spiritual mysticism, stay out of trouble, and leave running the church to certified religious professionals. This is why most sons are not interested in the Church. Real Christian men don't want to be passive pew-warmers.

Our sons – all of us – need a more biblical vision, of a militant church that serves Christ 24-7, and needs all of its men. Once our sons know that the church is a militant organization for discipleship and an instrument of cultural dominion, they take a greater interest in its proper functioning. They become interested in knowing systematic theology. They begin to take on the masculine character of the reformer who will preserve truly important doctrines, practices, and purposes of the church.

Doing this faithfully is not easy. It is the stuff of heroism. It is the kind of life that might get a man killed. Many men have died heroically for this cause in the past. This true, rugged Christianity will captivate boys' hearts, imaginations and obedience. Our sons must know that they are in the midst of a pivotal historic moment. They are an important part of history. The church needs them.

How can fathers help their sons refute the lies of the day?

Benjamin and his brothers are often challenged to think about ways to refute common lies of their generation. Their father gives them occasional assignments to defend a doctrine or refute a philosophy with scriptural references and careful argument. Below are some of misleading statements and lies of present-day culture which can be refuted by Scripture, which speaks to every one.

- History is not important
- Greeks were cool and Secular democracy has always been the best kind of government
- Good civilizations had lots of schooling. Bad ones had Christianity.
- The Puritans were evil and represent the dangers of Christianity and Western civilization
- The law says you have to go to school and the smartest, richest people go to college because school credentials from the state are the measure of schooling and higher-order personhood.
- Scientific, statist social engineering is proof that man is evolving from cave/primitive organism status to physical and social perfection.
- Pop culture is proof that freedom is license and license is good.
- There is no certainty of objective meaning which can be known. Truth is relative rather than universal and absolute. Reality is little more than one's perspective.
- The curriculum is not religious, but neutral and secular.
- "Secular" is superior to "religious' in matters of statecraft and education.

- The state, sovereign over the family, is the only legal and the best teacher of children.
- The state has sovereign lawmaking powers, and only the state has the ability and responsibility to reform people and institutions for a better world.
- There is a proven body of knowledge at the state teacher college level that represents the one best way for all children to learn and become good citizens.
- State training and certification of teachers is mandatory for all teachers. Other teachers are inferior and/or illegal "non-experts".
- Children want to be in school with children of the same age, and are better off in school than at home with their families.
- For their own good and the good of society, children need the socialization of the school environment as early as they can get it, preferably in pre-schools and kindergartens.
- Success in life, and approval by the state, requires attendance in state schools, and full agreement with a state curriculum.
- Because education is so important to the state's agenda, and to the better world it is creating, a person's value is directly connected to the amount of state education he receives. His academic credibility also depends on his state credentials and licenses.
- The world is getting worse because it's supposed to be getting worse.
- Old-fashioned child training methods are outdated.
- For many reasons, small families are best,

and kids should be on their own as soon as possible.

- The safest course for our kids' success is to keep them as closely as possible to accepted paths of progress: school, sports, college, college degree, job, career, mortgage, pension…and whatever else is popular for today.
- The modern church, with all its diverse ministries, powerful media technologies and dynamic leaders, is quite spiritually advanced.
- The 'kingdom of God' is heaven, or the term might possibly refer to the Church.
- Christians don't need to be involved in politics. It's better if they're not.
- The Old Testament is no longer that relevant for religious life, or any other kind of life, either.
- Full-time religious life is primarily a clergyman thing.
- Most religions are okay, and it's politically dangerous to say Christianity is superior. Non-Christians cannot follow Christian precepts.
- A healthy caretaker government is necessary for the common good, especially if it's scientific and secular rather than religious.
- The government could be doing a better job in education.
- It's only fair that the rich should pay more than their fair share of taxes.
- The U.N. can solve the war-peace thing better than any independent nations ever will.

VOLUME 4: WARFARE

LEARNING ABOUT THE DISCIPLINES OF CONQUEST BY THINKING LIKE A GOOD SOLDIER OF CHRIST JESUS

SECTION ONE: WEAPONS

Why are men supposed to be the protectors of women and children?

In her article "When Mamma Wears Combat Boots," Jennie Chancey writes:

> "From cover to cover, the Bible is packed with stories, laws, commands, and examples of men laying down their lives to protect the innocent and the weak. Christ is, of course, our primary example, and He calls men to follow Him by sacrificing in order to cherish, nourish, and protect the ones under their charge. The Groom of Scripture does not hide behind the skirts of His bride. In fact, men in Scripture who hide behind women are roundly condemned for their cowardice (see the account of Deborah the prophetess in Judges 4)."

Ephesians 5 paints a picture of Christ's sacrificial love, and the parallel sacrificial love men are to show their wives:

> "Husbands, love your wives, even as Christ also loved the church, and gave himself for it; That he might sanctify and cleanse it with the washing of water by the word, That he might present it to himself a glorious church, not having spot, or wrinkle, or any such thing; but that it should be holy and without blemish. So ought men to love their wives as their own bodies. He that loveth his wife loveth himself. For no man ever yet hated his own flesh; but nourisheth and cherisheth it, even as the Lord the church: For we are members of his body, of his flesh, and of his bones. For this cause shall a man leave his father and mother, and shall be joined unto his wife, and they two shall be one flesh. This is a great mystery: but I speak concerning Christ and the church. Nevertheless let every one of you in particular so love his wife even as himself; and the wife see that she reverence her husband." (Eph. 5:25-33)

In the standard biblical laws of warfare, God commands that women and children are to be protected – according to the standard rules, even the *enemy* women and children (Deut. 20).

To what extent are we commanded to protect all the innocent?

The Sixth Commandment is well known as forbidding murder. However, implied in the commandment is also a command to prevent murder. As John Calvin explains:

"Besides, another principle is also to be remembered, than in negative precepts, as they are called, the opposite affirmation is also to be understood; else it would not be by any means consistent, that a person would satisfy God's Law **by merely abstaining from doing injury to others.** Suppose, for example, that one of a cowardly disposition, and not daring to assail even a child, should not move a finger to injure his neighbors, would he therefore have discharged the duties of humanity as regards the Sixth Commandment? Nay, natural common sense demands more than that we should abstain from wrong-doing.

And, not to say more on this point, it will plainly appear from the summary of the Second Table, that **God not only forbids us to be murderers, but also prescribes that every one should study faithfully to defend the life of his neighbor,** and practically to declare that it is dear to him; for in that **summary no mere negative phrase is used, but the words expressly set forth that our neighbors are to be loved**. It is unquestionable, then, that of those whom God there commands to be loved. He here commends the lives to our care. There are, consequently, two parts in the Commandment – first, that we should not vex, or oppress, or be at enmity with any; and, secondly, that we should not only live at peace with

> men, without exciting quarrels, but should also aid, as far as we can, the miserable who are unjustly oppressed, **and should endeavor to resist the wicked, lest they should injure men as they list.**"
> (John Calvin, ***Commentaries on the Four Last Books of Moses***)

Rushdoony summarizes:

> "But all men have, as Calvin noted, "the duties of humanity as regards the Sixth Commandment." If they do not seek to prevent [specific] injury, assault, or murder, they are themselves in part guilty of the offense committed. The unwillingness in many instances of witnesses to act in cases of assault or murder may mean no entanglement on earth, but it incurs a fearful entanglement and guilt before God."
> (R.J. Rushdoony, ***Institutes of Biblical Law***)

In Exodus 22:2-3, we read: "If a thief be found breaking up [in], and be smitten that he die, there shall no blood be shed for him. If the sun be risen upon him, there shall be blood shed for him; for he should make full restitution; if he have nothing, then he shall be sold for his theft."

Although theft was not a capital crime, in darkness an intruder's motives would be unclear, and could potentially include a threat to someone's life. In this verse we see that even this ***chance*** of someone's life being in danger justifies self-defense to the point of killing the intruder.

Is it necessary to be armed and know how to use weapons?

Jesus commanded, "But now, he that hath a purse, let him take it, and likewise his scrip: and he that hath no sword, let him sell his garment, and buy one." (Luke 22:36)

We also have the example of the Israelites rebuilding the wall of Jerusalem:

> "Those who built on the wall, and those who carried burdens loaded themselves so that with one hand they worked at construction, and with the other held a weapon. Every one of the builders had his sword girded at his side as he built." (Neh. 4:17-18).

We should remember Nehemiah's charge to the men:

> "Be not ye afraid of them: remember the Lord, which is great and terrible, and fight for your brethren, your sons, and your daughters, your wives, and your houses." (Neh. 4:14)

We also have this interesting line listed amongst the signs of judgment upon Israel during the time of Deborah and Barak:

> "They chose new gods; then was war in the gates: was there a shield or spear seen among forty thousand in Israel?" (Judg. 5:8)

Why do so many Christians think that guns are bad?

Do we have a moral obligation to own weapons? Is refraining from weapon ownership as bad as surrendering our weapons to the state?

At what age should a son be trained to handle arms?

Why is it in the best interests of tyrants to disarm the populace?

As was stated in the United Nations Conference on the Illicit Trade in Small Arms and Light Weapons in All its Aspects:

> "The proliferation of light weapons gives greatest cause for concern when they cease to be in the control of security forces and become the charge of sub-state actors

> and organizations. This is the point at which control is crucial."

Conquering armies have nearly always disarmed the conquered to prevent continued resistance. In 1 Samuel 13:19 and 2 Kings 24:14-16 we see examples of policies to disarm the whole nation, namely by the removal of blacksmiths. Most weapons require constant maintenance; without this, and the ability to manufacture new weapons, a society will be slowly disarmed even without a comprehensive confiscation program.
During the time the Philistines were oppressing the Israelites:

> "Now there was no smith found throughout all the land of Israel: for the Philistines said, Lest the Hebrews make them swords or spears: But all the Israelites went down to the Philistines, to sharpen every man his share, and his coulter, and his axe, and his mattock. ... So it came to pass in the day of battle, that there was neither sword nor spear found in the hand of any of the people that were with Saul and Jonathan: but with Saul and with Jonathan his son was there found." (1 Sam. 13:19,20,22)

Modern totalitarian States understand well the thinking of the Philistines. Consider these numbers submitted by Dr. Michael Billings:

In 1929, the Soviet Union established gun control. From 1929 to 1953, about 20 million dissidents, unable to defend themselves, were rounded up and exterminated.

In 1911, Turkey established gun control. From 1915 to 1917, 1.5 million Armenians, unable to defend themselves, were rounded up and exterminated.

Germany established gun control in 1938 and from 1939 to 1945, a total of 13 million Jews and others who were unable to defend themselves were rounded up and exterminated.

China established gun control in 1935. From 1948 to 1952, 20 million political dissidents, unable to defend themselves, were rounded up and exterminated.

Guatemala established gun control in 1964. From 1964 to 1981, 100,000 Mayan Indians, unable to defend themselves, were rounded up and exterminated.

Uganda established gun control in 1970. From 1971 to 1979, 300,000 Christians, unable to defend themselves, were rounded up and exterminated.

Cambodia established gun control in 1956. From 1975 to 1977, one million 'educated' people, unable to defend themselves, were rounded up and exterminated.

In the 20th century, over 56 millions people, unable to defend themselves because of gun control, were rounded up and exterminated by their governments.

Patrick Henry said, "Guard with jealous attention the public liberty. Suspect every one who approaches that jewel. Unfortunately, nothing will preserve it but downright force. Whenever you give up that force, you are ruined... The great object is that every man be armed.... Everyone who is able may have a gun."

SECTION TWO: BATTLE

Is man's natural desire to fight a good thing?

Any father that has watched his sons play has observed that boys seem to have a natural attraction to war and conflict – they almost seem to gravitate towards anything that resembles a weapon, or has the potential to be fashioned into one. Is this a sign of their sin natures that should be trained out of them? Or has God given men these in-born tendencies for a special reason?

The Christian life is characterized by battle, conflict and warfare, and the New Testament is replete with military terms used to describe our Christian duty. We are called "soldier[s] of Jesus Christ" (2 Tim. 2:3), we wield "weapons" to "war" against the antithesis (2 Cor. 10:4), and we are commanded to take up the "shield of faith," the "helmet of salvation" and the "sword of the spirit, which is the word of God..." (Eph. 6:16,17)

The key is that our love of conflict must be used for His glory, in the One Great Battle – the battle for His kingdom. When it is used for man's glory it manifests itself in the sinful ways that we see through history – in greedy conquests, immature clashes between nations, bloody revolutions, unlawful crusades, vengeful massacres and the glorification of battle and bloodshed for its own sake.

How should we teach our sons to channel their militant natures?

In Doug Wilson's words:

> "Men who follow Jesus Christ, the dragon slayer, must themselves become lesser dragon-slayers. And this is why it is absolutely essential for boys to play with wooden swords and plastic guns. Boys have a deep need to have something to defend, something to represent in battle. And to beat your swords into plows prematurely, before

> the war is over, will leave you plowing for those who kept their swords. The Christian faith is in no way pacifistic. The peace that will be ushered in by our great Prince will be a peace purchased with blood. As our Lord sacrificed Himself in this war, so must His followers learn to do. Our boys must therefore learn to be strong, sacrificial, courageous and good."

Is it spiritual to get involved in earthly conflicts?

David Chilton points out:

> "The Spiritual man is not someone who floats in midair and hears eerie voices. The Spiritual man is the man who does what the Bible says (Rom. 8:4-8). This means, therefore, we ***are*** supposed to get involved in life. God wants us to apply Christian standards everywhere, in every area. Spirituality does not mean retreat and withdrawal from life; it means ***dominion***. The basic Christian confession of faith is that ***Jesus is Lord*** (Rom. 10:9-10) – Lord of all things, in heaven and on earth. In terms of Christian Spirituality, in terms of God's requirements for Christian action in every area of life, there is no reason for retreat."
> (David Chilton, ***Paradise Restored***)

Proverbs 25:26 tells us, "A righteous man falling down before the wicked is as a troubled fountain, and a corrupt spring." (The NASB translates it as "a righteous man who gives way to the wicked...")

What is the antithesis?

The word antithesis comes from the Greek word ***antitithenai*** meaning, "to oppose," or "to set against."

After the fall, God set the seed of the righteous against the seed of the serpent – this is the great spiritual antithesis. All men decide at young ages, consciously or unconsciously, which side they are on.

Greg Bahnsen writes,

> "One has to make this basic choice in his thinking: to be set apart by God's truth or to be alienated from the life of God. It cannot be two ways. One shall be set apart, set against, or alienated from either the world or from the world of God. He either refuses to follow God's word or he refuses to follow the vain mind-set of the Gentiles. He distinguishes himself and his thinking either by contrast to the world or by contrast to God's word. The contrast, the antithesis, the choice is clear: either be set apart by God's truthful word or be alienated from the life of God. Either have "the mind of Christ" (1 Cor. 2:16) or the "vain mind of the Gentiles" (Eph. 4:17). Either "bring every thought into captivity to the obedience of Christ" (2 Cor. 10:5) or continue as "enemies in your mind" (Col 1:21). (Greg Bahnsen,)

Of course, though the spiritual battle begins in our hearts and minds, it does not end there. The battle rages around us in every sphere, and we must fight for victory in every sphere.

> "...expositors have too often limited the promise of victory to the institutional church, or even more radically, to the human heart alone. Where a man's heart is, there will be his kingdom. If his hope of victory is limited to his heart, then his concern will be drastically narrowed. He will worry about his heart, his personal standing before God, his own sanctification, and his relationship to the institutional church. He will be far less concerned about exercising disciplined authority in the so-called secular realm. It is difficult psychologically to wage war on a battlefield which by definition belongs to the enemy." (Gary North, ***Backward Christian Soldiers?***)

> "[Many churches] teach the defeat of Christian civilization in history...[that] evil men will triumph culturally in history.

> The church's gospel of salvation will never transform the world. It will at best produce besieged little groups of Christians, vainly struggling to keep from being overwhelmed."
> (Gary North and Gary DeMar, ***Christian Reconstruction***)

What kind of warfare are we to be engaged in?

"For we wrestle not against flesh and blood, but against principalities, against powers, against the rulers of the darkness of this world, against spiritual wickedness in high places." (Eph. 6:12)

According to this verse we are combating religious systems, principles and lies – this is a war of ideas. And we are fighting against ideas ***with*** ideas, overcoming falsehood with truth, and evil with good. (Rom.12:21)

The weapons of our warfare:

"...having your loins girt about with truth, and having on the breastplate of righteousness; And your feet shod with the preparation of the gospel of peace; Above all, taking the shield of faith, wherewith ye shall be able to quench all the fiery darts of the wicked. And take the helmet of salvation, and the sword of the Spirit, which is the word of God..." (Eph. 6:14-17)

We don't always fight back with military weapons, but we must have a militant mentality. Sometimes we do have to physically contend with flesh-and-blood ***people*** using physical force, but we must remember that it is the ideas, worldviews, and principles, that cause the conflict. It is ideas that spark wars, trigger revolutions, build nations, establish governments, put tyrants on thrones and take them off. It is ideas, not physical weapons that will ultimately overcome evil and win the war.

This is how we must prepare ourselves for battle: "Study to

shew thyself approved unto God, a workman that needeth not to be ashamed, rightly dividing the word of truth." (2 Tim. 2:15)

"For though we walk in the flesh, we do not war after the flesh: (For the weapons of our warfare are not carnal, but mighty through God to the pulling down of strong holds;) Casting down imaginations, and every high thing that exalteth itself against the knowledge of God, and bringing into captivity every thought to the obedience of Christ;" (2 Cor. 10:3-5)

What are the real battles?

Though all false ideas come from one source (the deceiver) and are never really new, they manifest themselves differently in every generation. Thus battle lines change and it takes wisdom to discern them. Here are a few of the most crucial battles of our generation:

- The battle for the headship of the father
- The battle for the definition of gender roles
- The battle for the definition of marriage
- The battle for the unborn
- The battle for the rights of parents for their children
- The battle for truth in the media and arts
- The battle for Christian scholarship and education
- The battle for true scientific and medical research
- The battle for God's law to be the law of the land
- The battle for the crown rights of Christ to be proclaimed from the dining room table to the pulpit to the White House

What are some imaginary battlegrounds that can distract men from the real battles?

The sports field is possibly the "imaginary battlefield" that has distracted more men from the real fight than any other. It has channeled men's focus and masculine energy away from the real war. Moreover, devotion to violent and meaningless sport can actually pacify and emasculate men. Just as endless laboring with no purpose connected to dominion can degrade men, warring for things that don't matter can debase men – as well as steal away their hearts and minds from the fights that do matter. Sports have become the opiate of men around the world, and the idol of many professing Christians.

Video games and computer games are another popular outlet for men's natural competitiveness and love of battle; an outlet which can dull their minds and pull them out of reality into a fantasy world.

We should exercise caution with any spiritually meaningless competitions, from racing to debating. We ***should*** value the activities that can sharpen our sons for the real fight, but also beware lest they take an inordinate hold on them.

How is law a form of warfare?

"In brief, every law-order is a state of war against the enemies of that order, and ***all law is a form of warfare.*** Every law declares that certain offenders are enemies of the law-order and must be arrested. For limited offenses, there are limited penalties; for capital offences, capital punishment. ***Law is a state of war;*** it is the organization of the powers of civil government to bring the enemies of the law-order to justice.

"...Since law is a form of warfare, it follows that there is a required continual barrier to peace with evil. Man cannot seek co-existence with evil without thereby declaring war against God. The law declares, speaking of Ammorites and Moabites, apparently in this case in their continued life in terms of their law-culture, 'Thou shalt not seek their peace nor their prosperity all thy days forever' (Deut 23:6). A law-order cannot escape warfare: if it makes peace in one area, it thereby declares war against another." (R.J. Rushdoony, ***Institutes of Biblical Law***)

What law?

The catalyst of man's fall was this promise by the serpent: "Ye shall be as gods, knowing [***or determining for yourselves***] what is good and evil." What Satan was offering was sovereignty: the ability to determine right and wrong, to make law rather than follow it.

This was the ultimate rebellion against God, Who commanded, "Thou shalt have no other gods before Me" (Ex. 20:3). As Rushdoony explains,

"Law is the word and will of a sovereign. As we have noted, the first edition of the Encyclopedia Brittanica (1771) defined law as 'the command of the sovereign power, containing a common rule of life for the subjects.' Scripture recognizes no human agency as a sovereign power; God is at war against all such claims. Both church and state are ministries under God, and the state and its rulers are, literally, a diaconate (Rom. 13:1-4), servants of the Lord. The state thus has no independent powers, only powers, or, more literally, a service, delegated to it by the triune God."

There can only be one Sovereign, and thus there is only one Law-giver. God alone can make the laws – not the voice of the people, or an oligarchy, or a political party, or any other would-be sovereign.

"If Christ is Lord, then Caesar must be Christ's minister and obey His word (Rom. 13:1-4; Phil. 2:9-11)." (***Ibid.***)

What is Statism, and why is it idolatry?

Statism is a rival religion that puts the government in the place of God – the exchanging of one Sovereign for another. In Old Testament times, the state-god was known as Moloch/Molech. The modern Moloch State assumes God's authority in "the preserving and governing of all His creatures and all their actions" (as the Westminster Shorter

Catechism describes God's own acts of providence). Known in America as the Welfare State or the Nanny State, its main characteristics are compulsory government schooling, high taxes, a socialistic welfare program, an entrenched bureaucracy, police-state powers, and an ever-growing body of laws and regulations.

In what ways have American Christians paid service to Moloch instead of God?

How did Statism gain so strong a hold in America?

It is the Church that allows the State to grow outside of its bounds. Gary North explains,

> "The State needs pastors who preach a theology of defeat. It keeps the laymen quiet, in an era in which Christian laymen are the most significant potential threat to the unwarranted expansion of state power."
> (Gary North, ***Backward, Christian Soldiers?***)

Christian men have allowed themselves to become apathetic and passive in the knowledge that the professional clergy will take care of them in the spiritual world, as the Nanny State takes care of them in the secular world.

Rushdoony observes:

> "It is not an accident that the rise of Arminianism coincided with the rise of the modern state. Arminius warred against the doctrine of the necessitating God. Man's freedom required, he held, deliverance from such a God. To abolish necessity from theology is not to abolish necessity but to transfer it to another realm, and the state was progressively freed from God's necessitating power to become Hegel's god walking on earth, a this-worldly necessitating power."
> (R.J. Rushdoony, ***Sovereignty***)

"God's basic social institution is the family, to which God's law entrusts all the basic powers in government except the death penalty, which is reserved to the state. The control of children, of property, of inheritance, of education, and of welfare belong to the family. The basic functions of government are personal and familial responsibilities under God. Moreover, if men will neither tithe ***nor be responsible, it is because they are slaves and wish to be governed rather than to govern***." (*Ibid*., emphasis added)

SECTION THREE: ARMIES

Is it ever right to disobey a State order?

All earthly authority is limited, because all earthly authority is under God. When the command of another authority comes into conflict with the commands of God, we must say, as Peter did, "We ought to obey God rather than men" (Acts 5:29).

> "Law is inseparable from sovereignty; every word from a sovereign power is a binding word. Logically, there can only be one sovereign, and He is the Lord God of Scripture. ...To deny His laws in favor of another set of laws is to deny His doctrine in favor of a rival system. It is also a denial of His sovereignty in favor of another."
> (R.J. Rushdoony, ***Sovereignty***)

If an earthly authority tries to make us deny His sovereignty in favor of its own, and His laws in favor of its own, resistance becomes not only a right but a duty.

> "All law is religious in nature, and every non-biblical law-order represents an anti-Christian religion. But the key to remedying the situation is not revolution, nor any kind of resistance that works to ***subvert*** law and order."
> (R.J. Rushdoony, ***Institutes of Biblical Law***, emphasis added)

What are the grounds for lawful resistance?

One of the most influential documents in the history of government and freedom, Samuel Rutherford's ***Lex Rex*** ("The Law and the King," or "The Law is King"), examined the government's role as "the minister of God to thee for good" (Rom. 13:4), and the people's duties to that government. He concludes that resistance is lawful on these grounds:

> "Arg[ument] 1: That power which is obliged to command

and rule justly and religiously for the good of the subjects, and is only set over the people on these conditions, and not absolutely, **cannot tie the people to subjection without resistance, when the power is abused to the destruction of laws, religion, and the subjects.** But all power of the law is thus obliged, (Rom. xiii. 4 ; Deut. xvii. 18-20 ; 2 Chron. xix. 6 ; Ps. cxxxii. 11, 12; lxxxix. 30, 31; 2 Sam. vii. 12; Jer. xvii. 24, 25,) and hath, and may be, abused by kings, to the destruction of laws, religion, and subjects. The proposition is clear.

1. For the powers that tie us to subjection only are of God.
2. Because to resist them, is to resist the ordinance of God.
3. Because they are not a terror to good works, but to evil.
4. Because they are God's ministers for our good, but **abused powers are not of God, but of men, or not ordinances of God; they are a terror to good works, not to evil; they are not God's ministers for our good.**

Arg[ugment] 2: That power which is contrary to law, and is evil and tyrannical, can tie none to subjection, but is a mere tyrannical power and unlawful; and if it tie not to subjection, it may lawfully be resisted. But the power of the king, abused to the destruction of laws, religion, and subjects, is a power contrary to law, evil, and tyrannical, and tyeth no man to subjection: wickedness by no imaginable reason can oblige any man. Obligation to suffer of wicked men falleth under no commandment of God, except in our Saviour. A passion, as such, is not formally commanded, I mean a physical passion, such as to be killed. God hath not said to me in any moral law, Be thou killed, tortured, beheaded; but only, Be thou patient, if God deliver thee to wicked men's hands, to suffer these things." (emphasis added)

What are the lawful means of resistance?

In *Lex Rex*, Samuel Rutherford outlines three forms of lawful resistance, in order:

- First resort: Legal protest by appeals and reminders to the government
- Second resort: Fleeing from tyranny
- Third resort: Self-defense

Is war ever legitimate?

Not only does God frequently depict Himself as a "man of war" or "mighty in battle" (Ex. 15:3-9; Isa. 42:13, Ps. 24:8, Deut. 32:41-42), but He also commanded Israel to go into battle; assisted valiant men such as Joshua, Gideon and David in their warfare; and in His laws gives detailed instruction on how to righteously wage war (Deut. 20:1-20).

Although war is terrible, because of sin, war is at times a necessary means of overcoming evil. In his ***Biblical Law***, H.B. Clark summarizes:

"According to the Scriptures, 'there is no peace unto the wicked' (Isa. 48:22; 57:41), and it is futile to cry 'peace, peace, when there is no peace' (Jer. 6:14). If men would have peace, they must 'seek first the kingdom of God, and His righteousness' (Isa. 32:17), and there can be no lasting and universal peace until 'righteousness and peace have kissed each other' (Ps. 85:10). There shall be peace when 'the inhabitants of the world...learn righteousness.' It is 'in the last days' (Isa. 2:2) and when 'the Lord alone shall be exalted' (Isa. 2:11) that – '...the nations ... shall beat their swords into ploughshares, and their spears into pruning-hooks: nation shall not lift up sword against nation, neither shall they learn war any more' (Isa. 2:4)."

Until that time, war can be the righteous response to evil, as long as it is justly begun and righteously conducted. According to God's requirements for righteousness,

Rushdoony explains, "If warfare is to punish and/or to destroy evil, the work of restoration requires that this be done, that an evil order be overthrown, and, in some cases, some or many people be executed." (R.J. Rushdoony, ***Institutes of Biblical Law***) He writes:

> "Similarly, physical resistance, whether in the form of warfare or personal resistance to murderous attack, or the attempts of evil men to overwhelm us, is a godly stand and by no means wrong. In an evil world, such resistance is often necessary; it is an unpleasant and ugly necessity, but not an evil. David could thank God for teaching him to war successfully (II Sam. 22:35; Ps. 18:34; 144:1). In an evil world, God requires men to stand in terms of His word and law.
>
> "Warfare is a part also of a sinful order, but no less right under godly circumstances, and the right of the sword is by no means withheld because war belongs to the state of sin. Hardly an aspect of our lives can be separated from this sinful order in any full sense, but the law [of God] speaks to covenant-keepers in a sinful world, not to men in heaven."

When is war legitimate? What constitutes a just war?

Here is a summary of the biblical principles of just war, taken from Rev. William Einwechter's "A Christian Perspective on Just War":

- ***The war is conducted by legitimate civil authority.***
- ***The war is based on a just cause.***
- ***The war is waged with right intention.***
- ***The war is undertaken only as a last resort.***
- ***The war is fought on the basis of a reasonable chance of success.***
- ***The war has the establishment of a superior peace as its goal.***
- ***The war is waged with proper discrimination between combatants and non-combatants.***

The just causes of war, mentioned in Point 2, are generally the defense of life, liberty, and property against evil aggression. Rev. Einwechter summarizes just cause as "…for the purpose of defending life and property, vindicating justice, and reestablishing peace. A just war is a response to evil; it is an act of defense against international criminal activity (as defined by God's law); it is a resistance to lawlessness and a terror to evildoers."

Rushdoony makes this observation:

> "…the normal purpose of warfare is defensive; hence, Israel was forbidden the use of more than a limited number of horses (Deut. 17:16), since horses were the offensive weapon of ancient warfare. Thus, still another general principle appears: since war is to be waged in a just cause only, and, normally, in defense of the homeland and of justice, the right of conscientious objection means that one has a moral right to refuse support to an ungodly war."

In Einwechter's words:

> "The just war doctrine rejects the mindless patriotism of "my country right or wrong" and challenges the citizens to make a moral judgment concerning the wars their nation fights. If a citizen believes that the war is unjust he needs to refrain from participation in or support of the war. …
>
> "In summary, there are three kinds of war that are just: (1) wars of defense against aggression; (2) wars to help and defend an ally…from aggression; (3) civil wars to overthrow rank tyranny and oppression by the rulers or to put down evil insurrection."

Would such a war be considered a religious war?

Rushdoony writes:

> "In surveying military laws, we find that, ***first***, when wars are fought in terms of a defense of justice and the suppression of evil, and in defense of the homeland against an enemy, they are a part of the necessary work of restitution or restoration, and they are therefore spoken of in Scripture as ***the wars of the Lord (Num. 21:14). The preparation of the soldiers involved a religious dedication to their task (Josh. 3:5). ...it is not enough for the cause to be holy: not only the cause, but the people of the cause, must be holy, both spiritually and physically."***
>
> (R.J. Rushdoony, ***Institutes of Biblical Law,*** emphasis added)

This is why General George Washington issued these orders to his troops at Valley Forge:

> "The Commander-in-Chief directs that Divine service be performed every Sunday at 11 o'clock, in each Brigade which has a Chaplain. Those Brigades which have none will attend the places of worship nearest to them. It is expected that officers of all ranks will, by their attendance, set an example for their men. While we are zealously performing the duties of good citizens and soldiers, we certainly ought not to be inattentive to the higher duties of religion. To the distinguished character of Patriot, it should be our highest Glory to laud the more distinguished Character of Christian. The signal instances of Providential goodness which we have experienced and which have now almost crowned our labors with complete success demand from us in a peculiar manner the warmest returns of gratitude and piety to the Supreme Author of all good."

His first General Order upon taking command of the Continental Army in 1775 states:

> "The General most earnestly requires, and expects, a due observance of those articles of war, established for the Government of the army, which forbid profane cursing, swearing and drunkenness; And in like manner requires and expects, of all Officers, and Soldiers, not engaged on actual duty, a punctual attendance on divine Service, to implore the blessings of heaven upon the means used for our safety and defense".

On hearing a report that some of the men had been swearing, he sent out the following order:

> "The general is sorry to be informed that the foolish and wicked practice of profane cursing and swearing — a vice little known heretofore in the American army — is growing into fashion. Let the men and officers reflect 'that we can not hope for the blessing of heaven on our army if we insult it by our impiety and folly.' "

What does it mean to be part of a "house"?

Scripture often uses the word "house" to refer to family, generally in a multigenerational sense. A familiar example is Joshua 24:15: "And if it seem evil unto you to serve the LORD, choose you this day whom ye will serve...but as for me and my house, we will serve the LORD."

Rushdoony explains, "The ***house*** was an entity to which the various persons and ***generations*** belonged. It was an on-going fact, so that men did not think of the ***house*** as the nuclear family but as the past, present and future generations. (R.J. Rushdoony, ***Systematic Theology***)

The house was a dynasty that extended far into past and far into the future, and the accumulated wisdom, character and spiritual capital of these dynasties was an important part of the estate. This gave sons context, and an inheritance more valuable than money. As Rev. William R. Inge said, "The proper time to influence the character of a child is about a hundred years before he is born."

VOLUME 5: DOMINION

LEARNING THE DISCIPLINES OF FAITH THROUGH ENTREPRENEURIAL FAMILY LIFE WITH A FATHER

SECTION 1: STEWARDSHIP

What does dominion really mean? What would godly dominion in a nation look like?

The *first* command that the Lord gave mankind is what theologians call the "Dominion Mandate":

> "Be fruitful, and multiply, and replenish the earth, and subdue it: and have dominion over the fish of the sea, and over the fowl of the air, and over every living thing that moveth upon the earth." (Gen. 1:27b,28)

This mandate was repeated in another form, as His *last* command before He ascended into heaven:

> "And Jesus came and spake unto them, saying, All power is given unto me in heaven and in earth. Go ye therefore, and teach all nations, baptizing them in the name of the Father, and of the Son, and of the Holy Ghost: Teaching them to observe all things whatsoever I have commanded you: and, lo, I am with you alway, even unto the end of the world. Amen." (Matt. 28:18-20)

The earth is the Lord's, and all it contains (1 Cor. 10:26), and He calls us to exercise godly dominion of the nations under Him, in His name, as his *vicegerents* on the earth. A vicegerent, according to the Websters 1828 dictionary, is one "Having or exercising delegated power; acting by substitution, or in the place of another." Rushdoony explains,

> "Of Christ we are told that He is 'the head of all principality and power' (Col. 2:10), or, in the words of the Berkeley Version, 'the head of all princedom and authority.' This means that in Christ we are to claim every domain for Him and as His, and to exercise the authority of His law-word in every sphere. One such sphere is the natural world around us, and the earth beneath our feet. All things must be developed in terms of His dominion mandate. The development of agriculture and of technology, of

mining, horticulture, and all related disciplines, is a religious duty. The earth must be utilized to develop God's covenant mandate."
(R.J. Rushdoony, *Systematic Theology*)

What are the differences between today's picture of a macho "dominion" man, and the biblical picture of a manly dominion man? Do we point out to our sons the difference between what is good and what is not?

R.C. Sproul, Jr. says, "I see my life in terms of challenge, quest, warfare and adventure. That's what men do. This reflects the outward call of the dominion task. Men go into the jungle and turn it into a garden. Men are by nature conquerors, which is why it makes such perfect sense that God calls us to this task. In Him we are more than conquerors. The difference is that we do this for Him, rather than for ourselves. Dominion is all about conquest; that's what we're made for. Men live for a cause, and this is the cause, the crusade to which we have been called – to make manifest the reign of Jesus Christ."
(R.C. Sproul, Jr., *Bound For Glory: God's Promise For Your Family*)

Dominion is an inescapable fact of man's nature and relation to the world. Men are by nature dominion men – the question is, what kind of dominion are they taking? Godly dominion isn't despotic domination, nor is it destruction. It isn't Nazi-ism or barbarism. It is what cultivates and civilizes the world, and carries out the original order of the One Who made the world. The mandate for righteous dominion under God is what keeps man's natural desire for conquest from becoming power-hunger, blood-lust, or the love of spoil.

Are we doing all we can to preach the true gospel? How can we be doing more?

It is in Satan's best interests to keep Christians ineffective. One misunderstanding that has historically neutralized

Christians is an unbiblically narrow definition of "the gospel." Many believe the gospel we were commanded to preach is limited to "the Good News," the Four Spiritual Laws, the Sinner's Prayer, or at most, all the red words in the New Testament.

When Jesus, on the other hand, commissioned us to spread the gospel, He told us to "**teach** [make disciples of] all nations, baptizing them in the name of the Father, and of the Son, and of the Holy Ghost: **Teaching them to observe all things whatsoever I have commanded you**: and, lo, I am with you alway, even unto the end of the world. Amen." (Matt. 28:18-20)

The gospel we are to preach includes "all things whatsoever I have commanded you," which means the entire canon of Scripture. It means discipleship as well as conversion.

When Jesus chose the word "gospel" to describe our message to the nations, the word was already rich with meaning for that generation. At the time of Caesar Augustus' birth, it meant **"the formal announcement of the divine savior king."** The word was also used to indicate **the complete body of all Caesar's precepts, laws, decrees, edicts and proclamations**. This is what "the gospel" means – which is why Jesus often referred to the gospel as "the gospel of the kingdom of God" (Mat. 4:23, 9:35, 24:14, Mark 1:14). When we use the phrase "the Gospel of Jesus Christ," we must always be referring to His complete authority and rights as King of kings.

Our duty, therefore, is to teach entire nations to observe Christ's commandments, precepts, laws, decrees, edicts and proclamations. If the real gospel was preached worldwide, we would see cultural overhaul.

What does it mean to train our children to be successful?

What is the standard of success? For most, "success" means "fitting in," financial success, material accumulation, state accreditation, public recognition, popularity, accolades, and the approval of peers. This is not the biblical definition of success. The approval of God is the success we should seek. Insofar as our sons fear God, keep His commandments, and teach others to do the same, they have succeeded – and we have succeeded as parents.

> "But seek ye *first* the kingdom of God, and his righteousness; and all these things shall be added unto you." (Mat. 6:33)

It has been said, "We should not train our children to succeed. We should train our children to succeed us." One hallmark of true success is that each generation goes further than the generation before.

How should Christians view money and wealth?

Money is not evil. The *love* of money, for its own sake, is a root of all *kinds* of evil (1 Tim. 6:10). The love of God, and the desire to use every available resource to advance His kingdom, is a righteous desire. Using the resources He gives us, profitably, is also praised in Scripture. In the parable of the talents, the Lord illustrated the giving of servants hard assets as a test of how well they would use them, and rewarded the profitable stewards, with His favor *and* additional resources.

> "Then came the first, saying, Lord, thy pound hath gained ten pounds. And he said unto him, Well, thou good servant: because thou hast been faithful in a very little, have thou authority over ten cities." (Luke 19:16,17)

Money can be one effective tool to support and advance the work of the Kingdom, if it is used wisely and selflessly. The key principle is that His servants must invest it for *His* ends, not their own.

Rushdoony writes: "Wealth is a legitimate goal only towards establishing and furthering God's covenant and its dominion mandate. This is very clearly stated in Deuteronomy 8:18: 'But thou shalt remember the Lord thy God: for it is he that giveth thee power to get wealth, that he may establish his covenant, which he sware unto thy fathers, as it is this day.' It is a sin to believe, 'My power and the might of mine hand hath gotten me this wealth' (Deut. 8:17). God's covenant requires the godly use by all of their land, wealth, and abilities." (R.J. Rushdoony, *Systematic Theology*)

G. Ernest Wright explains the Deuteronomy passage further: "Wealth here is not by natural right; it is God's gift. Yet man must beware of the terrible and self-destructive temptation to deify himself which comes with it." (G. Ernest Wright, *Deuteronomy*)

What are some practical biblical safeguards against being corrupted by money?

Clearly, money is a dangerous blessing and must be used carefully. A godly man protects himself from the dangers of wealth by remembering, first, the source of wealth (from God, and not our own strength) and second, the purpose of wealth (for His glory, and not our own gratification).

How do we make sure that we are saving up an inheritance for our children, rather than accumulating wealth that God will need to confiscate, to bestow on more faithful servants?

Proverbs 13:22 warns: "A good man leaveth an inheritance to his children's children: and the wealth of the sinner is laid up for the just."

The Bible describes wealth as one of the rewards for the house of the righteous.

> "Praise ye the LORD. Blessed is the man that feareth the

LORD, that delighteth greatly in his commandments. His seed shall be mighty upon earth: the generation of the upright shall be blessed. Wealth and riches shall be in his house: and his righteousness endureth for ever." (Psa. 112:1-3)

List some of the blessings that make a man truly "wealthy." Do your children know what true wealth is?

Wealth can include more than pecuniary assets. The rich blessings of God that can rightly be considered "wealth" sometimes consist of deeper things, such as children, a virtuous wife, wisdom, or a godly legacy.

Is poverty more holy than wealth?

Two popular but heretical doctrines of wealth have confused Christians on this subject. "Poverty Theology" teaches that poverty is inherently more virtuous than wealth – in fact, is the only acceptable state for a Christian, wealth being inherently worldly, evil and corrupting everyone who possesses it. It is largely based on a misunderstanding of the parable of the rich young ruler. The idea of poverty and asceticism as being more holy has been around since before the time of Plato, but today it has been infected with modern socialism, and the idea that it would be more loving to everyone if all finite wealth was equally distributed.

Of course, this contradicts the Biblical doctrine that "The labourer is worthy of his reward," (1 Tim. 5:18) and "if any should not work, neither should he eat." (2 Thess. 3:10)

Is it selfish for some people to be wealthy when there are others who have less?

It is a fallacy that there is a finite, set amount of wealth in the world, that if one person gains, other people must lose. Columnist P.J. O'Rourke points out, "Wealth is not a pizza, where if I have too many slices you have to eat the Domino's box. In a free society, with the rule of law and property rights, no one loses when someone else gets rich." One man's hard work and profit always benefits the entire economy. One man's poverty cannot be blamed on another man's wealth.

Applying this on an international scale, theologian and economist Gary North writes,

> "...long-term poverty is always a sign of God's curse. The so-called underdeveloped societies are underdeveloped because they are socialist, demonist, and cursed. Any attempt to blame the poverty of the underdeveloped world on the prosperity of the West is absolutely wrong. This is the old Marxist and socialist line. It blindly fails to acknowledge the wrath of God on demonic, tyrannical, and socialist tribal cultures. There are too many books written by ostensible Christian scholars, who are in fact outright socialists and Marxists hiding behind a few out of context Bible verses, that attempt to make Christians feel guilty for their prosperity in the face of the "Third World's" poverty." (Gary North, *Unconditional Surrender*)

Should we be seeking wealth?

The "Prosperity Gospel" is another doctrine that has compromised Christians. It is generally a form of baptized materialism, often driven by superstar preachers who teach that the path to being financially blessed is to "tithe" lots of money to superstar preachers.

In this gospel, wealth is to be gotten by the manipulation of God, rather than by honest toil, the means *He* prescribed: "Wealth gotten by vanity shall be diminished: but he that gathereth by labour shall increase" (Pro. 13:11); or by honestly entreating His favor for its own sake.

This presumptuous doctrine is sometimes referred to as "name-it-and-claim-it" – we will receive certain blessings if we perform certain prayers or actions, treating God like a giant cosmic vending machine. It seeks to put the power in man's hands rather than God's, as though we can guarantee certain outcomes from Him by certain actions of ours.

Humble Christians should know that we cannot demand God's blessings, and we cannot coerce them with our own "good deeds." Our place is to humbly entreat His favor, and be content with whatever He sends us.

What attitude should we be teaching our families to have toward money?

Christians may be called to seasons of poverty. Whatever the life God has ordained for us, Paul taught us the attitude we are supposed to have toward wealth: "I know both how to be abased, and I know how to abound: every where and in all things I am instructed both to be full and to be hungry, both to abound and to suffer need." (Phil. 4:12)

The NASB renders it, "I know how to get along with humble means, and I also know how to live in prosperity; in any and every circumstance I have learned the secret of being filled and going hungry, both of having abundance and suffering need."

Charge your sons before God as Moses did. They must remember that God blesses entire families and culture based on the obedience of present and even previous generations. We cannot manipulate God. But we can prepare our hearts for the chastening or blessing that comes from our disobedience or obedience. When obedience is rewarded, pride can come, then greed, then the forgetting of God's commands.

"Beware that you do not forget the LORD your God by not keeping His commandments and His ordinances and His statutes which I am commanding you today; otherwise, when you have eaten and are satisfied, and have built good houses and lived in them,and when your herds and your flocks multiply, and your silver and gold multiply, and all that you have multiplies, then your heart will become proud and you will forget the LORD your God who brought you out from the land of Egypt, out of the house of slavery. He led you through the great and terrible wilderness, with its fiery serpents and scorpions and thirsty ground where there was no water; He brought water for you out of the rock of flint. In the wilderness He fed you manna which your fathers did not know, that He might humble you and that He might test you, to do good for you in the end. Otherwise, you may say in your heart, 'My power and the strength of my hand made me this wealth.' But you shall remember the LORD your God, for it is He who is giving you power to make wealth, that He may confirm His covenant which He swore to your fathers, as it is this day." (Deut. 8:11-18)

Are we experiencing God's judgments today, for our nation's pride and materialism?

We read in Scripture that if we break covenant with God, He promises to bring His lawsuit against us, and scourge us (Heb. 12:6) with judgment until we repent and turn again to Him. Rushdoony writes,

"When man is faithful to His Covenant Lord, the blessings of God come upon him and overcome him, in the city and in the field, and in his coming out and his going in. If, however, man is disobedient to God and His law, he is accursed in every area. As man is blessed, the earth and the weather are blessed; as man is accursed, so too is the earth and the weather.

"There is thus an essential relationship between man and the earth, a symbiosis which rests on man's relationship with God. This relationship rests on man's communion with God, or man's lack of communion. Man cannot step out of harmony with God without experiencing disharmony and conflict in all his other relationships." (R.J. Rushdoony, *Systematic Theology*)

Leviticus 26 and Deuteronomy 28 contain detailed warnings of specific grievances and judgments that accompany them, many of which we are already seeing in our nation.

SECTION TWO: MARRIAGE AND DEBT

How are we seeing the family fall apart?

As the family goes, so goes the world. The gradual disintegration of the family caused society to fall apart. It is a vicious cycle: as Western civilization continues to crumble, it further weakens whatever vestiges of family life remain. This process wasn't accidental, either – as Doug Phillips has said, "The defining crisis of our generation is the *systematic annihilation* of the biblical family."

God's enemies recognize the power of a biblical home, and it is in their best interests to make families weak and dysfunctional. In the last century, we've seen the re-definition of marriage. We've seen almost half of all marriages end in divorce. We've seen mothers pushed into the work-force. We've seen every medium of our day used to mock the father-figure. Perhaps most chilling, we've seen the murder of millions of babies, as parents the world over reject the fruit of the womb.

All generations have their defining crises. This is ours – the systematic annihilation of the biblical family. This is the crisis our sons have inherited. They need to know that one of the most important things they can do for the Kingdom is help rebuild the institution of the family – starting with their own.

What should we be teaching our sons about marriage and starting families?

Central to the dominion mandate is the command to be fruitful and multiply, to fill the earth and subdue it (Gen. 1:27b). Godly marriages are thus the cornerstone of dominion work. In preparing our sons for marriage and for leading families of their own, we must teach them the biblical purpose of marriage.

Quoting from *So Much More*, by Anna Sofia and Elizabeth Botkin,

"Marriage is about dominion. It's about filling the earth and subduing it. Marriage is about two people of different abilities and roles becoming one flesh, sharing one life and one vision, so that the two will complement each other and complete each other. It's about restoring the rib to the side of man so that the two are whole, finished, fulfilled. Only when they are united can the two represent them image and glory of God together. As a unit, the husband and wife can be fully effective, working together in s specially ordained dynamic life purpose – establishing the kingdom on God's terms for God's glory. ...

"God created the man and woman to be together. Together, they are an earthly image, a constant reminder, of the union of Christ and His Church, and will obey God's command to raise up a godly seed (Mal. 2:15). When God created humankind, He created them male and female, and then and there established the institution of male-female life-long unions and multigenerational dynasties. This is the heart of society. This is the heart of the dominion mandate. This is the heart of marriage as God created it." (*So Much More*)

Is it healthy for young men to think about marriage?

Fathers should be teaching their boys to plan for marriage from a young age, so these young men will have an appreciation for marriage that will govern all they do, including the way they enter into relationships.

They will not see other young people as playmates in an endless adolescence, but will respect all other young people as potential mates in other good marriages, and they will respectfully evaluate friendships in light of this.

A responsible son will not waste his time in reveries about marital bliss, but will pray for his future bride and be alert for one young woman who can be his life partner. He will not begin trifling friendships with young women or view single young women as part of a network of permanently casual "relationships." He will pray for all his acquaintances that they too find and discern the right matches for their marriages.

What qualities should we be teaching our sons to look for in potential wives?

We must teach our sons what to look for in godly wives, starting from the time they are very young. Our sons need wives who are very wealthy in terms of character. Here is one *sample* list of character requirements for a potential wife:

- She should be a Christian who has entrusted her heart to Christ and to her father.
- She should love the Word and study it diligently.
- She should have an expansive vision for family, marriage and motherhood.
- She should be extremely well educated, but not by the world's standard.
- She always endeavors to make others feel comfortable
- She is prepared to be a homemaker and has a strong desire to be a homemaker.
- She has a strong desire to be a mother of as many children as the Lord wants to give.
- She has a gentle and quiet spirit.
- She can cook for 5 or 50.
- She dresses and acts modestly and femininely.
- She is a gracious speaker.
- She is willing to make her husband her life's work.
- She is willing to be led and discipled by her husband.
- She has an excellent relationship with both her father and mother.
- She has fostered good relationships with her siblings.
- She has an interest in history and church planting.
- She has developed a comprehensive biblical worldview.

What kind of character must our sons have to be worthy of this kind of young woman?

There are fathers of young ladies who have been raising their daughters to desire marriage to young men of substantial spiritual capital. Many of these fathers will use lists like this one to help their daughters evaluate suitors:

Foremost, of course, the man must be regenerated.
He must be a mature Christian, who consistently demonstrates the fruit of the spirit.
He would demonstrate the character qualities of an elder, as listed in 1 Tim. 3 and Tit. 1:5-9.
He must be the kind of man that I can respect and joyfully submit to.
He should have a vision for ministry to which I can devote my life.
He will love God with all his heart, soul, mind, and strength.
He should love me, just as Christ loved the Church and gave himself for her, but I want him to love Christ more than he does me.
He should treat me with honor and respect, but should not be afraid to be the active head of the family.
He should be respectful and considerate of all women in general.
He should be a protective, loving father to our children and will want as many as God is pleased to give us.
He should be a leader and not a follower, and will speak out boldly for what is right.
He should be devoted to prayer.
He should be habitually eager to learn from Scripture, to be challenged by Scripture, and to seek God through Scripture.
He will delight in meditating on God's Law, as King David did.
He should have a solid Christian worldview, and the moral clarity and moral courage that goes with it.
He will have the discernment to recognize the traditions of men, the elementary principles of the world, bad philosophy and empty deception.
He will not be taken captive by false doctrines but will consult Scripture before forming doctrinal judgments.

He should be able to understand and evaluate historical and current affairs with a thoroughly biblical perspective.
He should seek the companionship of wise men and limit his association with lesser men.
He should be respected and esteemed wherever he goes; his character should be irreproachable.
He should be teachable and able to teach with humility.
He should be well educated in the right ways and for the right reasons, and will not place undue value on the world's academic credentials.
He should have a vision for his family that is multi-generational.
He should be able to fit in comfortably with my family and have a respectful relationship with my father.
He should be a good steward of all that God has given him (e.g. time, money, spiritual gifts).
He will have a respect for God-given authority.

How can we do better at raising our sons to be truly qualified suitors?

We should provide them with the tools of character, entrepreneurialism, and a vision for Christian living. Debt is a dangerous foundation on which to begin a marriage. We should help our sons become financially responsible, and, where possible, teach them the skills they will need to support their families. There was an old saying: "He who does not teach his son the law and a trade teaches him to be a fool and a thief." It is a great blessing for a son to have his father teach him to be an entrepreneur with a vision not just to make money but to build culture, the economy, a strong Christian dynasty and worldwide Christian civilization.

What is courtship?

Disclaimer: *A strict courtship formula is not the one solution to the challenges of marrying well. There is no strict formula for courtship found in the Bible.*

Christian courtship is an advanced cultural custom of a disciplined, Christian civil society that protects the covenantal institution of marriage by providing a short period of time for a girl to objectively determine her willingness to follow the man approved by her father to be her husband, and for the young man to confirm his ability to love and disciple the young lady.

Fathers have a God-given, protective authority over well-prepared daughters to give them carefully to worthy husbands with the consent of the daughters so that the suitor and daughter are equally yoked in a covenant representing a purposeful relationship with a multigenerational dominion objective.

What is wrong with 20th century dating?

Since WW II, **dating** has been the dominant cultural custom for establishing temporary man-woman relationships in the post-Christian west. The custom is not driven by commitment to family bonds but rather a hedonistic flight from family responsibility. It is the selfish, recreational pursuit of personal gratification through serial relationships with other damaged, emotionally promiscuous people who have weak family relationships and little intention of marriage. The gratification sought is usually emotional attachment for girls and, often, physical conquest for boys. In some circles it represents serial promiscuous fornication. In others it represents the pursuit of casual, non-committal relationships in the pursuit of prolonged adolescence and an avoidance of marriage.

What are the biblical examples of the principles that go into making marriages?

Betrothal, Engagement — Exod. 22:16-17; Deut. 22:23-29; 2 Sam. 3:14; Matt. 1:19f

Covenants — Gen. 21:27-31; 31:48ff; Num. 30:2; Deut. 23:21-23; Josh. 9:18-20; Zech. 8:17; Mal. 3:5; Gal. 3:15

Dowry/Bride Price — Gen. 34:11-12; Exod. 22:16-17; 1 Sam. 18:25; 2 Sam. 3:14

Patriarchal Protection — Num. 30:3ff; Deut. 22:21; Ps. 36:7; 2 Cor. 11:2

Father Giving Bride — 1 Cor. 7:36-38; Lk. 20:34-35; Exod. 22:17

Romantic Emotions/Touching — Gen. 20:4,6; 26:8; Exod. 22:16f; Deut. 22:23f; Ruth. 2:9; S. of Sol.1-3; Matt. 5:28; Rom. 13:14; 1 Cor. 7:1; 1Thess. 4:6; 1 Tim. 5:1-2

Wedding — Ps. 45:13ff; S. of Sol. 3:6-11; Mal. 2:14; Matt. 22:2ff; 25:1ff; Jn. 14:2f; Rev. 19:7ff

What does the Bible say about debt?

The Bible does not teach that incurring short-term debt is always a sin, but it is clear that caring so little about our freedom in Christ that we would willingly enslave ourselves to another, to serve two masters – because we care *so* much for the things of the world – is a sin.

However, Romans 13:8 says, “Owe no man any thing, but to love one another: for he that loveth another hath fulfilled the law.”

In addition, Psalm 112:5 tells us, “A good man sheweth favour, and lendeth: he will guide his affairs with discretion.”

Though borrowing may not be a sin, it is clearly not the general practice of the responsible man – it is his place to lend.

Some have asked whether being an employee is a form of debt. Working for Christians can be a win-win scenario for employer and employee, both of whom can be acting with carefully invested entrepreneurial interests, neither taking advantage of the other. The employee can gain more than a wage compensation; he can gain the experience and mentoring needed to become a business owner in his own right. The employer can gain the faithful assistance of an honest worker to make his business succeed. Such a contractual relationship benefits both parties, and both go above and beyond the terms of the contract in doing all things as unto the Lord. (Col. 3:17)

Both employer and employee are investing equally valuable assets in the covenantal relationship, and both parties acknowledge this fact. Both, in obedience to Christ, can be working toward gaining more freedom to be slaves of Jesus Christ. (1 Cor. 7:21)

What are "the cultural disciplines which predispose men to attitudes of slavery"?

Example: Debt, entertainment, welfare, government "benefits," feminism, etc.

SECTION THREE: COLLEGE

What kind of education should we desire for our sons? How important is education?

We should desire for our sons to be extremely well educated, in the right ways and for the right reasons. We should desire to see them thoroughly trained for the practical duties of manhood and dominion work. "A complete and generous education," as John Milton defined it, is "that which fits a man to perform justly, skillfully, and magnanimously all the offices, both private and public, of peace and war."

Is college the place to give our sons that kind of education?

Honest analysts of the education system are concluding that the answer is no. Both on an academic and practical level, graduates are coming out with educations that would be considered sub-par, by the biblical and historical standard.

Christians all over America persist in thinking that colleges have the monopoly on higher learning, higher qualifications, and proper training. Our children, and their educations, have suffered for this mistake of ours. The historic fact is that *the best-educated men of history have always been* ***autodidacts***. "Autodidact" is a Greek word, meaning "self-teacher" – **a man who takes responsibility for his own education.**

This should come as no surprise to us. Just as it was discovered that home education produced superior results to state education, it is being proven that often, disciplined, self-motivated youth who study on their own are better equipped for life in the real world than their college-grad counterparts.

Are there things our sons could get at college that we think they wouldn't get without it?

Some point out that there are *some* worthwhile benefits to the college experience – practice interacting with all kinds of people, incentive for focused study, having to stand up for one's faith, having to analyze other worldviews, learning to "make decisions as adults," etc.

These are certainly a vital part of a complete education. However, if college is the first time our children experience these, *then we've done an inadequate job as parents.* Our children should be veterans in all these areas long before they reach college age. Our job as parents is to provide them real-life opportunities for this. There are certainly socially inept youth, undisciplined, unmotivated, and untested, for whom college might prove a genuine kick in the pants. This is a sad indictment on the young people and their families – not a justification for college. It should be a call to parents to remedy the problem – not a call for the state to do it for them.

How is the academic quality of the modern university curriculum?

Increasingly, their academic rigor and integrity are becoming a joke. "Why would any self-respecting boy want to attend one of America's increasingly feminized universities?" wrote George Gilder, author of *Men and Marriage*, in *National Review*. According to Gilder, the American university is now a "fluffy pink playpen of feminist studies and agitprop 'herstory,' taught amid a green goo of eco-motherism . . ."

How useful is the practical, vocational training?

As far as practical, vocational training goes, college has been proven less effective than other higher-education alternatives. To use the MBA degree as an example,

> "In articles published in Business 2.0, *National Post*, the *Chicago Sun-Times*, and the *Chronicle of Higher Education,* Stanford Business School Professor Jeffrey Pfeffer stated that you may be just as successful in your career if you do a two or three week boot camp on business basics instead of a two-year MBA. Professor Pfeffer analyzed 40 years of research on the economic value of an MBA

> degree. He concluded that it does not guarantee a successful career or a higher salary." (Dr. Gary North, "Donald Trump vs. The Mandarins")

College can have certain success in preparing your sons to be wage-slaves, but not to be entrepreneurs. Gary North, Ph.D. and economics expert, writes, "If there is a kiss of death for entrepreneurship, it is the outlook of the liberal arts departments of an American university." He concludes, "It is better to get on-the-job training in a mid-sized business noted for its entrepreneurship than it is to earn an MBA. It is better to come under the influence of a manager who has prospered in a growing company than a professor of business administration." (Gary North, "Donald Trump vs. The Mandarins")

Is a college degree necessary for our sons' success?

One argument for college is the belief that men need that college degree to get a good job to make enough money to take care of a family. There is debate as to how helpful degrees even are in getting jobs working for other men. As Isaac pointed out, in many fields they are becoming obsolete – or worse, proof of lack of self-motivation.

We also need to beware of overvaluing the accreditation of men. If we knew more about the accrediting agencies and their standards, would we prize their stamp-of-approval as highly?

Dr. Gary North reveals,

> "The decision to accredit or not accredit is backed up by the Federal government and the states, which have granted a monopoly to the regional accrediting agencies to license institutions of higher education. These accrediting agencies are unknown to the public. They operate in near-secrecy, yet they control entry into a $270 billion a year industry: American higher education.

> "This has all been done behind the scenes. I am aware of no book on the history of the accreditation agencies, with their links back to Rockefeller's General Education Board (1903), itself deliberately shrouded in anonymity by its creator." (Dr. Gary North, "Donald Trump vs. The Mandarins")

In a different article, he further explains:

> "If the degree-granting system were really honest – if it were not run by a cartel – then accredited college degrees would be offered to any person who could pass the same exams that the tuition-paying students also have to pass. If the student could learn the material on his own, but pass the standardized exams, then he would get the degree.
>
> Accrediting associations don't allow this. Why not? Because it would bankrupt hundreds of colleges that are protected from true competition by the accrediting associations. It would wipe out the colleges' tuition system, real estate system, and low teaching load system." (Dr. Gary North, "The Dorm Key Ritual")

Biblically, what is the difference between reaching out to those in darkness, as disciple-makers, and placing ourselves under them, as learners?

The Bible makes many comments about associating with and studying under ungodly men, both things that the college experience requires. Here are just a few:

"Blessed is the man that walketh not in the counsel of the ungodly, nor standeth in the way of sinners, nor sitteth in the seat of the scornful. But his delight is in the law of the Lord, and in His law doth he meditate day and night." (Psa. 1:1,2)

"Enter not into the path of the wicked, and go not in the way of evil men. Avoid it, pass not by it, turn from it, and pass away." (Pro. 4:14,15)

"I have not sat with vain persons, neither will I go in with dissemblers. I have hated the congregation of evil doers; and will not sit with the wicked." (Psa. 26: 4,5)

What should we recommend to sons who have an interest in a technical field, such as medicine or engineering?

There are some technical fields that require intensive specialized training only available, for the present, at universities. At the moment, many of these fields are controlled bureaucratically, inefficiently, and unbiblically. Many say they need to be reformed; in truth, they need to be replaced.

We have two main options before us. We can study under experts of the system, be approved and certified by them, and then work with them in perpetuating their existing system. Or – we can step back and see if there is a more effective and courageous alternative. Those who drift through life accepting everything expose themselves to dangerous positions. Reformers step back and ask questions. The answer is, yes, there are alternative courses.

Professionals both inside and outside the legal and medical industries are contemplating arrangements that would take licensure out of the hands of the government, weaken the monopolies of insurance and pharmaceutical cartels, and make the professions honest and decentralized. Young people with interest in fields such as law and medicine should research the growing alternatives, rather than perpetuate the current system by their participation. It may make life more challenging for them, but they will bequeath a better situation to their children. We should be training our sons to think long-term – not to choose what seems best for them, but to choose what would be best for their descendents.

We have the privilege of living in a time of transition – transition from an anti-Christian society to a more Christian one. As the vanguard, we must see that infiltrating the problematic systems will not fix the problem. We need to end the systems, and provide a replacement. We need to create new accreditation systems and new industries. This is entirely possible – not tomorrow, or even next year, but it can be done. This is another reason we must teach our sons to think multigenerationally.

We should be thankful for the times God chose to put us in, the battles He has given us to fight. As Abigail Adams wrote to her son, John Quincy:

> "These are times in which a genius would wish to live. It is not in the still calm of life, or in the repose of a pacific station, that great characters are formed. The habits of a vigorous mind are formed in contending with difficulties. Great necessities call out great virtues."

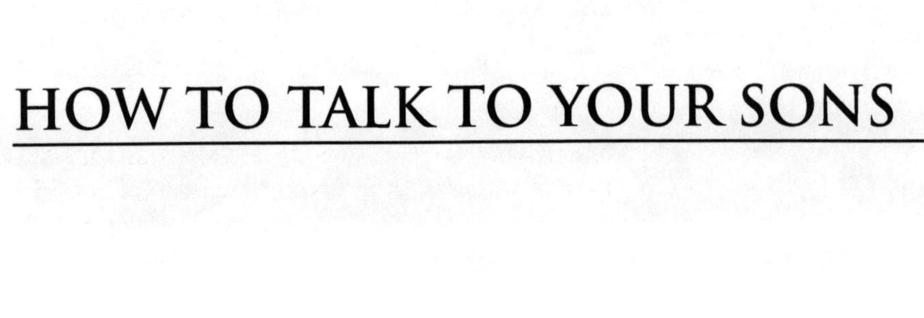

HOW TO TALK TO YOUR SONS

SECTION ONE: COURAGEOUS TALK

What subjects characterize the conversations we have with our sons?

The strength of a nation can be measured by the caliber of the conversations between its men. In America today, "manly" conversation is often characterized by inappropriate remarks about women, boastful or covetous banter about toys (cars, computers, boats etc.), and heated arguments relating to sports. Some of today's American men have replaced manliness with macho-ism. Macho-ism can be understood as a version of manliness that is dominating and aggressive in a self-centered and power hungry way. It can seem strong and tough on the outside, but at its core it is essentially self-serving, weak and cowardly. Real biblical manliness, on the other hand, is self-sacrificing and courageous in its pursuit to bring all things under the dominion of Christ, not itself. Macho-ism hates commitment, dodges responsibility and evades confrontation with the pressing needs and problems in the real world; biblical manliness seeks responsibility and embraces the hardships and duties that come from being committed to the cause of Christ.

The macho man will avoid conversations that remind him of his responsibilities, but the real man will initiate them. The macho man talks about how he fills his time, the real man talks about how he redeems his time.

What was manly conversation like 300 years ago when America was stronger?

In sharp contrast to the childish banter that occurs between many of the men in modern-day America were the discussions that occurred in humble New England taverns during America's founding:

> "The inevitable talk was of politics, religion, and trade. Some of the denizens talked 'tolerably well,' remarked one visitor who made the rounds of such establishments

> in 1744, and displayed 'that curiosity which was characteristic of the American rustic everywhere.' In one New Jersey tavern, he overheard a discussion about Physics, in another, an argument about sacred history between two Irishmen, a Scot and a French Jew. At Saybrook Ferry, Connecticut, some 'country rabble' came in and, to his surprise, began talking theology—'so pointedly, in fact, about justification, sanctification, adoption, regeneration, repentance, free grace, original sin and a thousand other such pretty chimerical knick-knacks one would have thought they had had done nothing but study divinity all their lives.'"
> (Benson Bobrick, *Angel in the Whirlwind)*

How do we teach our sons about duty and responsibility?

At the heart of every conversation between a father and son there should be the presupposition of man's moral responsibility to God. This should be reflected in the subject matter and caliber of our discussions.

> "...the doctrine of providence means that, at every moment, every man confronts the living God. His response, whether for good or evil, is a personal and moral response. Man is inescapably a responsible creature."
> (R.J. Rushdoony, *Systematic theology)*

Teaching our sons to be responsible means teaching them how to live each moment, how to confront every moral test, and how to take every thought captive.

But our sons need to understand that their responsibility as Christian men extends further than their own personal accountability: as fathers they will be required to look after the spiritual and physical well-being of their families, and furthermore, as His image bearers they have a duty to assume responsibility for their world as they take dominion and disciple the nations.

> "Responsibility for us is then not a chore but the key to a world of knowledge, holiness, righteousness, and dominion under God as His image bearers."
> (R.J. Rushdoony, *Systematic Theology)*

As men who embrace our responsibility as fathers, we must not be afraid to bring up the subjects that are really tough. Three of the hardest and most important are: **RIGHTEOUSNESS, SELF-CONTROL,** and **THE JUDGMENT TO COME.**

How can we obtain true righteousness?

True righteousness can only be obtained by knowing God and conforming every detail of our lives to His commandments and precepts. King David was described as a man whose heart was wholly devoted to the Lord (1Kings 11:4). It is plain from reading the Psalms that David sought the heart of God through a diligent study of His Law.

> O how love I thy law! it [is] my meditation all the day. (Psa. 119:97)

> Blessed [are] they that keep his testimonies, [and that] seek him with the whole heart. (Psa. 119:2)

The only way to really know God is to know what He has said about Himself in His Word.

> "'Acquaint now thyself with Him, and be at peace: thereby good shall come unto thee' (Job 22:21). 'Thus saith the Lord, let not the wise man glory in his wisdom, neither let the mighty glory in his might, let not the rich glory in his riches: but let him that glorieth glory in this, that he understandeth, and *knoweth me*, that I am the Lord' (Jer. 9:23,24).

> "A spiritual and saving knowledge of God is the greatest need of every human creature.

> "The foundation of all true knowledge of God must be a clear mental apprehension of His perfection as revealed in Holy Scripture. An unknown God can neither be trusted, served, nor worshipped...
>
> "Something more than a theoretical knowledge of God is needed by us. God is only truly *known* in the soul as we yield ourselves to Him, submit to His authority, and regulate all the details of our lives by His holy precepts and commandments. 'then shall we know, if we follow on (in the path of obedience) to *know* the Lord' (Hosea 6:3). 'If any man will *do his will*, he shall know' (John 7:17). 'The people that do *know* their God shall be strong" (Dan. 11:32).'" (Arthur Pink, *The Attributes of God)*

How can a father teach self-control?

Every boy is a sinner and needs a father who will confront him in his sin, who will teach him about the nature of sin, and who will help him to master sin.

One of the best ways a father can teach his son self-control is to confess his own sins to his son and to demonstrate genuine repentance and a palpable "turning away" from them. A father can also talk to his sons about the temptations that all men (including he) face in this world, describing some of the mistakes he made, how he conquered pet sins and resisted temptations. Our sons must see us grow and progress as we master sin ourselves.

What does your son need to know about the Judgment to come?

Every boy needs to be reminded that he will die. Every father must explain to his son the sober reality that all his actions, both great and small, will have eternal consequences. On the Day of Judgment he will give account for every idle word (Matt. 12:36), the value of his life work will be revealed through fire (1Cron. 3:13), and he will be recompensed for his deeds, whether good or bad (1Cron. 3:13).

What kind of mission should a father have?

Fathers who have difficulty knowing how and what to communicate to their sons would do well to start with developing a family mission. Fathers and sons who are united by a common purpose and goal will never lack conversation topics. Too many sons are perishing from a lack of vision. "Where [there is] no vision, the people perish: but he that keepeth the law, happy [is] he." (Prov. 29:18) As fathers we need to be giving vision to our sons, but we can't do this if we have no vision of our own. Christian fathers must:

- Embrace an international mission (Matt. 28:20)
- Pursue a specific local mission
- Articulate a family mission

How can we articulate this mission to our families?

Throughout the history of Christendom, Christian fathers and leaders have used maxims, mottos, mission statements, and rallying cries, to cast vision and give direction. The leaders of the Reformation gave us "Semper Reformanda" and the five Solas. The Scottish Presbyterians gave us: "For Christ's Crown and Covenant." We fathers can learn from their example and adopt mission statements for our families. The Scriptures have given us many:

> "Whom we preach, warning every man, and teaching every man in all wisdom; that we may present every man perfect in Christ Jesus…" (Col. 1:28 – the NASB translates it as "We proclaim Him, admonishing every man and teaching every man with all wisdom, so that we may present every man complete in Christ."
>
> "Go ye therefore, and teach all nations, baptizing them in the name of the Father, and of the Son, and of the Holy Ghost: Teaching them to observe all things whatsoever I have commanded you." (Mat. 28:20)
>
> "…[But] as for me and my house, we will serve the LORD." (Jos. 24:15)

SECTION 2: HONEST TALK

How many worldviews do we preach to our sons?

"...And, ye fathers, provoke not your children to wrath: but bring them up in the nurture and admonition of the Lord." (Eph. 6:4)

One of the things that will provoke a son to wrath is when a father simultaneously instructs him in the admonition of the Lord and in the admonition of the world. In our conversations with our sons we must not indicate that we serve two masters or two worldviews. If we have truly rejected the world's wisdom, then we cannot speak in the world's terms presupposing their lies to be true.

What are some of the world's lies?

Some of the most common lies that have infiltrated our instructions to our sons pertain to security, education, the meaning of success and the purpose of money. Our teaching must echo the teachings in Scripture with the same clarity and consistency.

> "No man can serve two masters: for either he will hate the one, and love the other; or else he will hold to the one, and despise the other. Ye cannot serve God and mammon. Therefore I say unto you, Take no thought for your life, what ye shall eat, or what ye shall drink; nor yet for your body, what ye shall put on. Is not the life more than meat, and the body than raiment?" (Matt. 6:24-25)

> "But seek ye first the kingdom of God, and his righteousness; and all these things shall be added unto you." (Mat. 6:33)

Many fathers teach their sons to hold fast to the principles and sentiments of these passages, but unconsciously discourage them from putting them into practice.

What should our goals for our sons be?

"Draw nigh to God, and he will draw nigh to you. Cleanse your hands, ye sinners; and purify your hearts, ye double minded." (James 4:8)

Our sons do not belong to us but to God, and the law that we teach them must be His, not ours or the world's. With this in mind, we must train them up to be the sons that their heavenly father can be proud of. Our goal is not to raise them to hear the applause of the public, but to hear God's voice saying: "Well done, [thou] good and faithful servant: thou hast been faithful over a few things, I will make thee ruler over many things: enter thou into the joy of thy lord." (Matt. 25:21)

There are 21 main reasons why we fail to consecrate our sons:

6. We neglect to turn our hearts firmly toward the children.
7. We are distracted by or are serving mammon.
8. We are not watching and shepherding our sons' hearts.
9. We don't shield them from danger and defilement.
10. We don't see them as potential warriors.
11. We don't see them as potential leaders or patriarchs.
12. We don't see them as God created them, as future prophets, priests and Kings.
13. We don't set them apart for service to God.
14. We don't include them in our life's major plan.
15. We include them in the world's plan.
16. We don't model Christian duty.
17. We don't nourish their souls.
18. We don't train guide or train their character.
19. We don't warn them about sin.
20. We don't teach them solid theology and good discernment.
21. We don't teach them to think.
22. We cast them adrift without true provisions.

23. We turn our boys over to the experts because we do not realize we are fully qualified to prepare them for life.
24. We don't introduce them to good allies.
25. We don't expand their intellectual curiosity.
26. We don't talk to them enough.

If we have failed our sons, it's time to admit it to ourselves, to God, and to them.

"If we confess our sins, He is faithful and righteous to forgive us our sins and to cleanse us from all unrighteousness." (1 John 1:9)

What are a few things we may need to confess to our sons?

I have weaknesses, and I have not been looking to Christ alone for strength.
I've been captive to the traditions of men.
I haven't been thinking right and doing right whatever the cost.
I've been afraid of social criticism.
I haven't been leading decisively.
I haven't been gentle with your mother.
I haven't insisted on obedience as the family authority. I haven't disciplined you justly.
I haven't cleaned up the media toxins in our home.
I haven't been leading to get us out of debt bondage and a slave mentality.
I haven't represented patriarchal vision the way a father must.

Is corporal punishment loving or unloving?

One of the most telling indications of a father's neglect and lack of love is a son who is undisciplined, unruly or out of control.

> "The solution offered in Scripture is the rod. "Do not withhold correction from a child, for if you beat him with a rod, he will not die. You shall beat him with a rod, and deliver his soul from hell" (Prov. 23:13,14). Fathers are given the tool of corporal punishment to shape the behavior of their children and also the attitude of the heart. The rod represents the father's authority (and hence the mother's as well, since she shares his authority as his helper). It is the parents' means of physically restraining the bad behavior of their children and bringing them in to line with God's standards.
>
> " 'Child abuse' would be defined from the biblical perspective as a *failure* to use the rod. Those who distain its use do not love their children enough to save their souls form hell!"
> (Philip Lancaster, *Family Man, Family Leader*)

The rod was prescribed to fathers as a tool with which to represent God's justice and loving chastisement; with it we teach our sons that there are consequences for their actions and that disobedience will be punished. Ultimately, we use the rod to teach them the concept of law, the eternal consequences for its violation, and the need for true repentance before God.

The modern belief that corporal punishment is barbaric and unloving is very popular even among Christians, but the Scripture says:

> "He that spareth his rod hateth his son: but he that loveth him chasteneth him betimes." (Prov. 13:24)

By our example, what are our sons learning about the meaning of the word "father"? What are some characteristics they are learning to associate with the word "father"?

The purpose of this series is to impress on fathers the life-changing and world-changing significance of father-son conversations. But what speaks the loudest of all to our sons is the testimony of our actions and deeds. The most important thing we can do as fathers is to model Christian character to our sons and to become men that they can respect and emulate.

"In all things shewing thyself a pattern of good works: in doctrine shewing uncorruptness, gravity, sincerity…" (Tit 2.7)

The best inheritance that we can leave to our sons is a legacy of love for God's Word.

"…[B]lessed is the man that feareth the Lord, that delighteth greatly in his commandments.
His seed shall be mighty upon earth: the generation of the upright shall be blessed."
(Psa. 112:1,2)

DISCUSSION SHEETS

These pages can be photocopied or printed from PDF files included on the Father to Son DVDs or downloaded from www.westernconservatory.org

VOLUME 1: WORK

SECTION ONE: COMMUNICATION

Do we give our sons the kind of instruction that will guide them, preserve them, and give them light for the rest of their lives?

Do we provoke our children to wrath by never giving them the fatherly instruction Scripture commands them to heed?

How would we train our sons differently, if we considered that we are teaching them to train their sons?

What if we are not very good communicators? How can we become better?

How do we teach our sons to love Scripture?

What areas of our lives have we not yet conformed to Scripture? In what areas do other things dictate our opinions and decisions?

What should we learn from the story of Eli?

Do we let any things hold priority over our duties to our families?

What are some incisive questions for serious dads?

VOLUME 1: WORK

SECTION TWO: WORK

Why is work so important?

Is our own work connected to the biblical purpose of work?

Is work a result of the curse?

What influences may be teaching your sons that work is undesirable?

What is the difference between rest and leisure? Should we ever have leisure time?

Is boredom in our sons a problem?

What is the difference between boredom, and taking time for quiet reflecting and meditating?

To what extent is boredom a result of an inactive, disengaged mind, lack of interest in the world around us, discontent, and purposelessness, as well as a lack of something to do?

How can we kindle in our sons an interest in real things that will supercede an appetite for leisure and escapism?

How can we always help our sons understand the importance of every task we give them?

Are some kinds of work more spiritual than others?

What kind of tasks and assignments can we give our sons, to let them become part of the dominion-taking mission now?

Should men ever retire from their dominion work? How about taking vacations?

VOLUME 1: WORK

SECTION THREE: EDUCATION

What is education?

What is the purpose of education?

What kind of education should our sons have?

What is the difference between humanist education and Christian education?

How did the educational standards of John Milton's time compare with ours?

VOLUME 2: ADVENTURE

SEGMENT ONE: ADVENTURE

What part does adventure play in the Christian life?

Think of some examples of common adventures fathers and sons have, and how you can teach your sons to process each adventure.

What does it mean for a son to give his father his heart? What would it look like?

Do your sons understand your ways? Do they know what you believe about all the important issues of life? Make a list of some of the things you need to talk to your sons about this week.

What are some changes we need to make in our own lives, to make sure we are setting an honorable and respectable example to our sons? To make sure our ways are worthy of delighting in?

What snares do fathers need to vigilantly watch out for, that could steal their sons' hearts away? Make a list of outside influences that may need to be checked.

Why do fathers need to be leaders?

What are some ways men are leading badly in their families today?

What are some ways we can be more proactive in making opportunities with our sons?

What are a father's chief duties to his family?

What are some practical ways we can be preparing even young boys to protect, provide for and lead their future families?

Do your sons know why they are being educated?

Think of at least three academic disciplines you'd like to start helping your sons master now.

Do your sons already have academic interests and goals that you can be encouraging them in?

What lessons can we take from the example of Johann Wysse writing Swiss Family Robinson for his son?

What messages are we preparing to pass on to our sons? What kind of a legacy are we preparing for our sons?

VOLUME 2: ADVENTURE

SEGMENT TWO: WOMEN

What are some of the culturally popular views of women that we need to dispel to our sons?

How can we teach our sons to show honor to women? Discuss some practical ways they can cultivate and demonstrate respect.

What should we teach our sons about the dangers of women?

How does Scripture describe the marks of the "strange woman"? How can we train our sons to recognize her?

What is the danger of "strange women"? Why does Scripture warn young men away from them so strongly?

Why do women wield so great an influence over men? What weaknesses of ours make us so susceptible to their sometimes-ungodly sway?

What kinds of thoughts should we inspire our sons to think about the young women they see, to put temptation out of their minds?

How much should we teach our sons about girls and marriage while they're still young?

What qualities should we teach our sons to admire in women?

How do we train our sons to value these qualities in women?

What are some faults we should teach them to look out for?

A bad wife can drag a man down, and hold him back from going where the Lord wants him to go. What other things keep men from reaching the level they should?

VOLUME 2: ADVENTURE

SEGMENT THREE: HISTORY & VISION

How should we encourage our children to play?

What playthings and activities could encourage a godly masculinity in our sons?

What kinds of playthings and activities could foster the wrong attitudes in our sons?

What should we think about toy guns? Tinkertoys? X-boxes? GI Joes? Building tree-forts? Playing board games?

What positive lessons should we learn from the men of the 6th century? And what warnings can we take from their example?

Who are some good historical role models our sons should know? What are some great examples of Christian heroism they can strive to emulate?

What does it mean to be a prophet, priest and king for your family?

Have we been providing for our own in all the ways we should be?

What kind of example have we been setting to our sons?

If we could see our sons emulate us exactly with their own future families, would we be pleased with how they governed their homes? Would God be pleased?

Why is it important to teach our sons history? How can an understanding of history help us face the present?

What is the great end Christian men should be adventuring towards?

What does it mean to occupy until He comes?

Our sons need to understand the objectives they've been given as Christian soldiers. What are our marching orders, and what is the victory we fight for?

What are some practical ways this thinking will affect how we raise our sons?

We live on a battleground, not a playground. What does this mean?

VOLUME 2: ADVENTURE

SECTION FOUR: KNIGHTHOOD

How would keeping journals help us?

Is there one best way to journal?

Why must every man have messages?

What are some of our generation's crying needs?

What are some messages that we would really like our generation to hear?

If we could only give one message to this generation, what would it be?

What elements and concepts of knighthood do we need to transmit to our sons?

How should we train our sons to be gentlemen?

Why is the grandest adventure of all being a family man?

If we were exercising dominion in and through our homes, what would our homes look like?

VOLUME 3: WORSHIP

SEGMENT ONE: WORSHIP

What questions would you ask your sons to discern their spiritual condition?

What is the church legacy that our sons have inherited?

What is the definition of apostasy?

How might today's apostasy be described?

If this is the legacy of the 21st century church, how do we as Christian men need to be reforming it?

What does it mean to teach our sons to think like Reformers?

Are our sons at all attracted to the world? Do they wish to be part of it in any way?

Are our churches defaulting to the cultural norm, or setting the example for the world to follow?

Is there something inherently wrong with "contemporary?"

How have both models defaulted to contemporary cultural norms?

How have both models been perpetuated without careful analysis?

Do our sons have a proper understanding of Who God is, and who man is?

What gods do professing Christian men all too often serve? What other gods are we serving?

What is worship? Have we truly been worshiping God in the way that He requires?

What is the church?

How should churches train and mobilize "those whom Christ governs and who are therefore called to govern the earth under God"?

Should we train our sons to be clergymen or ministers?

VOLUME 3: WORSHIP

SEGMENT TWO: REFORMATION

How do we reform our own churches if there are some weaknesses?

Is it ever acceptable for families to leave churches?

What character should reformers always model to the body of Christ?

Are there different kinds of worship? What are they?

What does Semper Reformanda mean? What would it look like in our own lives?

What are some practices of the modern church that must be reformed?

What is the criteria of a church's success, if not numbers?

What is the sacred-secular distinction? Is it a biblical idea?

If there is no secular-sacred distinction, does this mean that every field of labor is a place for Kingdom work? That Christians are required to take dominion of them all?

VOLUME 3: WORSHIP

SEGMENT THREE: MUSIC

What is wrong with most worship services today?

How can we teach our sons what emotions are lawful or unlawful? How can we teach them to control their emotions biblically?

Do we know what kind of music our sons are listening to, and what affect it may be having on them?

What can we and our sons learn from the examples of men like Bach?

How do God's principles of order apply to other areas of creativity, such as architecture, graphic design, or filmmaking?

What are our sons learning from us about their worship and religious duties?

How can fathers help their sons refute the lies of the day?

VOLUME 4: WARFARE

SECTION ONE: WEAPONS

Why are men supposed to be the protectors of women and children?

To what extent are we commanded to protect all the innocent?

Is it necessary to be armed and know how to use weapons?

Why do so many Christians think that guns are bad?

Do we have a moral obligation to own weapons? Is refraining from weapon ownership as bad as surrendering our weapons to the state?

At what age should a son be trained to handle arms?

Why is it in the best interests of tyrants to disarm the populace?

VOLUME 4: WARFARE

SECTION TWO: BATTLE

Is man's natural desire to fight a good thing?

How should we teach our sons to channel their militant natures?

Is it spiritual to get involved in earthly conflicts?

What is the antithesis?

What kind of warfare are we to be engaged in?

What are the real battles?

What are some imaginary battlegrounds that can distract men from the real battles?

How is law a form of warfare?

What law?

What is Statism, and why is it idolatry?

In what ways have American Christians paid service to Moloch instead of God?

How did Statism gain so strong a hold in America?

VOLUME 4: WARFARE

SECTION THREE: ARMIES

Is it ever right to disobey a State order?

What are the grounds for lawful resistance?

What are the lawful means of resistance?

Is war ever legitimate?

When is war legitimate? What constitutes a just war?

Would such a war be considered a religious war?

What does it mean to be part of a “house”?

VOLUME 5: DOMINION

SECTION ONE: STEWARDSHIP

What does dominion really mean? What would godly dominion in a nation look like?

What are the differences between today's picture of a macho "dominion" man, and the biblical picture of a manly dominion man? Do we point out to our sons the difference between what is good and what is not?

Are we doing all we can to preach the true gospel? How can we be doing more?

What does it mean to train our children to be successful?

How should Christians view money and wealth?

What are some practical biblical safeguards against being corrupted by money?

How do we make sure that we are saving up an inheritance for our children, rather than accumulating wealth that God will need to confiscate, to bestow on more faithful servants?

List some of the blessings that make a man truly "wealthy." Do your children know what true wealth is?

Is poverty more holy than wealth?

Is it selfish for some people to be wealthy when there are others who have less?

Should we be seeking wealth?

What attitude should we be teaching our families to have toward money?

Are we experiencing God's judgments today, for our nation's pride and materialism?

VOLUME 5: DOMINION

SECTION TWO: MARRIAGE AND DEBT

How are we seeing the family fall apart?

What should we be teaching our sons about marriage and starting families?

Is it healthy for young men to think about marriage?

What qualities should we be teaching our sons to look for in potential wives?

What kind of character must our sons have to be worthy of this kind of young woman?

How can we do better at raising our sons to be truly qualified suitors?

What is courtship?

What is wrong with 20th century dating?

What are the biblical examples of the principles that go into making marriages?

What does the Bible say about debt?

What are "the cultural disciplines which predispose men to attitudes of slavery"?

VOLUME 5: DOMINION

SECTION THREE: COLLEGE

What kind of education should we desire for our sons? How important is education?

Is college the place to give our sons that kind of education?

Are there things our sons could get at college that we think they wouldn't get without it?

How is the academic quality of the modern university curriculum?

How useful is the practical, vocational training?

Is a college degree necessary for our sons' success?

Biblically, what is the difference between reaching out to those in darkness, as disciple-makers, and placing ourselves under them, as learners?

What should we recommend to sons who have an interest in a technical field, such as medicine or engineering?

HOW TO TALK TO YOUR SONS

SECTION ONE: COURAGEOUS TALK

What subjects characterize the conversations we have with our sons?

What was manly conversation like 300 years ago when America was stronger?

How do we teach our sons about duty and responsibility?

How can we obtain true righteousness?

How can a father teach self-control?

What does your son need to know about the Judgment to come?

What kind of mission should a father have?

How can we articulate this mission to our families?

HOW TO TALK TO YOUR SONS

SECTION TWO: HONEST TALK

How many worldviews do we preach to our sons?

What are some of the world's lies?

What should our goals for our sons be?

What are a few things we may need to confess to our sons?

Is corporal punishment loving or unloving?

By our example, what are our sons learning about the meaning of the word "father"? What are some characteristics they are learning to associate with the word "father"?

ALSO AVAILABLE FROM THE WESTERN CONSERVATORY

FATHER to SON
SIX-DISC DVD SET

This six-part DVD series is designed to provide fathers and future fathers with simple examples of manly discussion. Where does a dad begin? With the pressing issues that weigh on young minds, these informal, unrehearsed conversations between Geoffrey Botkin and his five sons show how it can be done.

Each episode tackles an age appropriate discipline of manhood and how it is developed with fathers. Each rich conversation is broken into short study segments, and the text of this book is provided as PDFs which can jump-start family or Bible-study discussions.

HOMESCHOOL DROPOUTS

The "first generation" home schooling movement is almost three decades old. It has been a stunning success. Even the most critical skeptics admit this. "But," they ask, "what about the second generation? Will the homeschool graduates do what their teachers did?"

This documentary examines the history of the movement and the character that will be required to sustain it into the second generation and beyond.

Made in the USA
Charleston, SC
02 March 2013